AGING

AND

OUR FAMILIES

Handbook for Family Caregivers

Donna P. Couper

Foreword by

Anna H. Zimmer

HUMAN SCIENCES PRESS, INC.

Library of Congress Cataloging in Publication Data

Couper, Donna P.
   Aging and our families: handbook for family caregivers.

   Bibliography: p.
   1. Aged—Home care—United States—Handbooks, manuals, etc. 2. Parents,
Aged—Home care—United States—Handbooks, manuals, etc. 3. Adult
children—United States—Handbooks, manuals, etc. I. Title.
HV1461.C73 1989   362.6'0973   88-8807
ISBN 0-89885-441-5

The production of this material was supported, in part, by a grant, number 90AT0309/
01, from the Administration on Aging, Department of Health and Human Services,
Washington, D.C. 20201. Grantees undertaking projects under government sponsor-
ship are encouraged to express freely their findings and conclusions. Points of view or
opinions do not, therefore, necessarily represent official Administration on Aging
policy.

© 1989 Human Sciences Press, Inc.
A Subsidiary of Plenum Publishing Corporation
233 Spring Street, New York, N.Y. 10013

Printed in the United States of America

AGING

AND

OUR FAMILIES

Handbook for
Family Caregivers

Dedicated to

JKP

FOREWORD

The two volumes that comprise <u>Aging and Our Families</u>, the <u>Handbook for Family Caregivers</u> and the <u>Leader's Guide to Caregiver Programs</u>, are designed as important links between the informal supports of family caregivers and the human service organizations that enable families to fulfill their chosen role in eldercare. The publications developed by Donna Couper are important additions to the practical and educational resources for care of the disabled elderly. These books are products of a project, funded by the Administration on Aging (AoA), of the Connecticut Department on Aging and the Travelers Center on Aging of the University of Connecticut. They should be broadly disseminated as valuable tools for both the formal and informal networks of service.

The decade of the 1980s was ushered in with long-overdue attention to the keystone of long-term care--the family caregiver. The demographic imperative of the rapid increase in the cohort of the old-old--those who depend most on family caregivers as they cope with chronic disability--was dramatically detailed in the Stone, Cafferata, and Sangl (1987) study "Caregivers of the Frail Elderly: A National Profile." Their data report that in 1982 approximately 2.2 million caregivers provided unpaid assistance to 1.2 million noninstitutionalized disabled elderly. Such statistics underscore the need to design services that support and supplement this family effort.

The <u>Handbook</u> and <u>Leader's Guide</u> build on the recommendations of earlier AoA model projects highlighting the need for education, skills training, and emotional support for family caregivers. (See Zimmer & Mellor, 1981; and Silverman, Brahce, & Zielinski, 1981.) Because parent care is now seen as a "Normative Family Stress" (Brody, 1985), a body of literature, curricula, handbooks, films, and videotapes geared to coping with that stress is fast developing. A review of the projects in the family caregiving programs of the Administration on Aging, National Institute on Aging, National Institute of Mental Health, Health Care Finance Administration, and Human Development Services shows extensive research, program development, and various media productions that aim to give caregivers the range of knowledge, skills, and understanding they so keenly need.

It is encouraging to note that the Connecticut project targeted the religious community, as well as social service and health care agencies, as the focal points for program development for caregivers. Having been invited to Connecticut's end-of-project conference, the results of this targeting was apparent to the many staff who participated. Reports of respite care, educational series, and support groups, as well as an increased sensitivity to caregiver needs reflected the goal of the project.

In 1978 we bemoaned the fact that there was no "Dr. Spock of eldercare." Since then, many titles have joined Barbara Silverstone and Helen Hyman's pioneer work, You and Your Aging Parent (1976), but family members still report that communication pertaining to this responsibility is hard to come by. Therefore, a handbook such as this--easy to read, well-organized, brief but informative--is most welcome. Above all, Donna Couper respects the underlying philosophy of recognizing the strength in family caregivers, and her work is indeed a tool to be used toward their empowerment.

Perhaps this philosophy is best stated in the Caregiver's Bill of Rights which was compiled by the Caregivers Network of the National Supports Program (cited in Zimmer & Mellor, 1981):

Caregiver's Bill of Rights

1. Right to live a life of one's own.
2. Right to choose a plan for caring.
3. Right to be free from any form of financial or legal coercion when choosing a plan for providing care.
4. Right to be recognized as a vital source of family stability.

These two volumes respect this Bill of Rights and are a confirmation of the underlying philosophy that caregivers are strong people committed to caring for their aged in the community as long as they can, and who need enabling services from the formal system to cope with the unavoidable stress they experience.

The Handbook addresses the caregiver's right to such information. For the family member or friend in the midst of years of caregiving, or about to take on an often stressful role, the Handbook will be most helpful. Attention is given to instrumental needs and emotional needs of both the care receivers and caregivers. Each part has a listing of activities and provides corresponding discussion outlines in the Leader's Guide. These can be valuable to caregivers, either individually, or in association with other family members, or as a program for an educational or support group.

The author's review of the literature in the Leader's Guide is complete, and is welcomed as the framework for the two books. A carefully selected bibliography for the informal caregiver and for the professional enabler is given in the Leader's Guide for each major segment of the Handbook. The Leader's Guide, concise and readily understood, becomes a tool for both caregivers and those who provide services to them. Although guidance for program planning is given, there is also identification of problem areas such as outreach to varied populations. Just as caregivers must learn they "can't go it alone," providers of service, especially those developing

Foreword

education and training or support groups, must involve different sectors of the community network.

The effort to form a meaningful partnership of informal caregivers and the formal service system is well served by these publications. Caregiving has indeed come of age when public grants produce such resources, and it is hoped that public policy will someday reinforce this trend.

Anna H. Zimmer
Director, Institute of Mutual Aid/ Self-Help in the Field of Aging
The Brookdale Center on Aging of Hunter College

References

Brody, E. M. (1985). Parent care as normative family stress, The Gerontologist, 25, 19-29.

Silverman, A. G., Brahce, C. I., & Zielinski, C. (1981). As parents grow older: A manual for program replication. Ann Arbor, MI: University of Michigan.

Silverstone, B. & Hyman, H. K. (1976). You and your aging parents: The modern family's guide to emotional, physical, and financial problems. New York: Pantheon Books.

Stone, R., Cafferata, G. L., & Sangle, J. (1987). Caregivers of the frail elderly: A national profile. The Gerontologist, 27, 616-626.

Zimmer, A. H. & Mellor, M. J. (1981, September). Caregivers make the difference: Final report (Administration on Aging Contract No. 02AM48). Community Service Society of New York.

INTRODUCTION

Aging and Our Families is about family members who look after or care for older adults. The primary caregiver in families is the one who is principally responsible for providing care or coordinating assistance for frail or disabled older family members. The caregiver may be a spouse, adult child, sibling, or other relative.

This Handbook for Family Caregivers is useful to family caregivers and to those who work with older families. Its purpose is to help individuals understand some of the psychological and emotional issues older families face. Practical ideas are suggested for strengthening support systems for primary caregivers within the family, among friends and neighbors, and through religious and community groups.

Clergy, social service providers, health care professionals, and employee-assistance personnel can use this handbook as a resource for primary caregivers and other family members. The activities listed at the end of each section are effective tools for small group discussions. A supplemental volume, Leader's Guide to Caregiver Programs, includes additional discussion questions for small group seminars and tips on how to organize and facilitate educational programs for caregivers.

Discussions of the issues faced by older families often raise questions, but do not always provide adequate answers to individual problems. No two situations are identical. Each situation varies, depending on the persons involved, the nature of their relationships, the time and place. Outside circumstances influence how one feels, thinks, and acts at any given moment.

Introduction

This handbook is not intended to provide answers to specific individual and family problems, but rather to help primary caregivers assess their family situations and identify possible alternatives. The suggestions are based on sound principles of human relations that have been helpful for others. Yet, it is in no way comprehensive--nor could it be.

Nurses, physicians, lawyers, social workers, counselors, family therapists, and members of the clergy are important resources for older families. Their expertise can lend valuable guidance in personal and relevant ways to specific concerns.

The information presented here is designed to help persons understand the needs of family members and identify ways to strengthen the support of both dependent older adults and their family caregivers. The book offers understanding, acceptance, and encouragement.

ACKNOWLEDGMENTS

The Handbook for Family Caregivers and an earlier version of the Leader's Guide to Caregiver Programs were developed as part of the Caregiver Information Project. This project, funded by the Administration on Aging, was a joint effort of the Connecticut Department on Aging and the Travelers Center on Aging at the University of Connecticut. The major goal of the project was to reach family caregivers through the help of concerned members of the religious, social service, and health care communities.

I am indebted to individuals at the Connecticut Department on Aging for providing me the opportunities to work in the area of elder family caregiving for the past several years. Appreciation goes especially to Alice Gilbert, Louis Goldblatt, Commissioner Mary Ellen Klinck, and Dr. Kevin Mahoney. I appreciate the efforts of Dr. Nancy Sheehan for making it possible to combine efforts with both the Connecticut Department on Aging and the Travelers Center on Aging.

Members of the Caregiver Information Project Advisory Committee were: Reverend Bob Casstevens, Joyce Hellerman, Carol LeSeur, Cathalee Johnson, Sister Rita Johnson, Reverend Phil Rider, Sister Mary Louise Rouleau, William Wasch, and Philip Weiner. Appreciation is extended to them for their review and suggestions. Thanks also go to Richard Meth, Dr. Lucille Nahemow, Dr. Vincent Rogers, Dr. Ronald Sabatelli, and Dr. Eugene Thomas of the University of Connecticut for their review of the material.

Lisa Marella and Richard Wilson provided essential support in the completion of this material as well as the training and research components of the Caregiver Information Project.

Acknowledgments

Fred Couper not only tolerated the extra hours this project necessitated, but meticulously edited this manuscript. Beverly Hynes-Grace was the friend to whom I turned for ideas and encouragement.

I am grateful to those persons from social service, health care, and religious organizations who participated in the Aging and Our Families training sponsored by the Caregiver Information Project. Together we learned and shared information. I am indebted to the family caregivers who have shared parts of their lives with me. Final appreciation goes to Norma Fox and the staff of Plenum Publishing for making this information available to more families.

CONTENTS

I

UNDERSTANDING THE SITUATION

Who **is** caring for frail and disabled older adults? What is the role of the family? How do different family members respond to the needs for physical and emotional support? Can family caregivers do **too** much? These are the questions addressed in Part I.

Chapter 1, "Aging: What It Means to Families," describes the response of most families to the increased dependency needs of their older members. Chapters 2 and 3 look at the special situations of husbands, wives, sons, and daughters. Chapter 4 discusses the often overlooked support siblings and friends offer. Chapter 5, "The 'Super' Caregiver," emphasizes some of the problems encountered when individual family members take on too much of the caregiving responsibilities. The activities at the end of this part are intended to help caregivers take a personal look at their own unique situations.

1

AGING: WHAT IT
MEANS FOR FAMILIES

Significant demographic changes are affecting families as both the numbers and proportion of older people increase. The number of older adults will continue rising substantially as the post-World War II "baby boom" generation reaches old age. The ratio of older adults to younger adults is also increasing. These trends raise concerns about our society's ability to provide for the needs of a growing older population.

An increase in life expectancy has also created substantial population increases among the "old-old," those people over 75 years old. Since the likelihood of chronic illness and disability increases with age, those over 75 are as a group most likely to need assistance.

Most older adults manage to live vigorous and independent lives. However, many require varying degrees of assistance. Needs of older persons may include physical, social, emotional and financial assistance. People living to advanced age often rely on help from family members, friends, and neighbors.

Contrary to popular myth, families do not "abandon" their older members. They are instead closely involved in providing a range of support needs. Families are the preferred source of assistance among older adults and contribute to the social, psychological, and physical needs of their older members. Although formal support provided by social service and health care agencies offers important services, family members are the major source of help for most older persons.

While caring for an older member affects everyone in the family, it does not affect each person equally or in the same manner. In most families, one person assumes the primary caregiving responsibilities, with other family members providing supportive assistance. The majority of primary caregivers are women: wives, daughters, or daughters-in-law. However, a growing number of primary caregivers are men. Social trends indicate that men will play more significant caregiving roles in the future.

While families are important voluntary resources for helping dependent older adults, they are often unprepared for the duties and stresses that accompany caregiving. Changes within older families cause ambivalent feelings and concerns. Most families want to do "the right thing," but are unfamiliar with and uncomfortable with the issues they face. Although most families respond to the needs of older members, it is not without difficulties. Demands on time, money, and energy are often great.

I had no idea it would be so awful. In less than a year, we helped my folks sell their house and move into a retirement apartment complex. Then Dad had to go to a convalescent home, leaving Mom alone in the apartment. He died short of two months in the nursing home. My brothers and I took care of the estate--mounds and mounds of paperwork--to make certain Mom would be able to live comfortably in her apartment. But her health and mind deteriorated so much that the manager of the apartments could not let her stay there any longer. Now she's living with me. . . . Managing all this on top of my job. . . . Sometimes I don't know if I'm coming or going.

The greatest stress for family caregivers is the emotional and psychological strain. Caring for a dependent older person involves making changes within the family. It usually includes reallocating household tasks; negotiating with siblings,

4

spouses, children, and other relatives; making major and routine decisions which affect family members of all ages. Particularly worrisome can be the reassessment of relationships--past, present and future--which occurs during difficult family times.

The actual tasks of caregiving depend mostly on the level of dependency of the older adult. However, the meaning given to caregiving depends mostly on the relationship of the caregiver and the older person. Adjustments in relationships must be made to accommodate increasing dependency needs. Family adjustments to these new situations take time, and the necessary transitions are not easy ones.

The following sections look at both the level of care and the nature of care as it affects the primary caregiver and the family.

2

HUSBANDS AND WIVES
AS CAREGIVERS

Many couples in old age share a long history of both struggles and joys. More than half of those over 65 years of age live in independent households with a spouse. Husbands and wives in later life usually fulfill important roles for each other. Their time spent together increases after retirement and after the children leave home. When a husband or wife becomes physically dependent because of declining health, the primary caregiver is most often the spouse with the better health condition.

Kinds of Support Given

The level of support from spouses varies with the partner's level of dependency needs. Assistance ranges from simple tasks such as planning a special diet, to difficult tasks such as helping with mobility. Difficulties increase for spouse caregivers as their own health deteriorates, sometimes brought on by the added stress and physical demands of caregiving. In some cases, both spouses have limiting health problems, but manage to compensate for each other's weaknesses.

The ease with which older men and women assume caregiving roles varies. Although women may be more accustomed to caregiving tasks, men in later life report participating more in general household tasks than they did in earlier years. The sharing in household responsibilities to the extent each is capable can contribute to the morale of both older husbands and wives.

Psychological and emotional changes of older men and women can influence their outlooks toward caregiving. Many women in later life become more independent and turn to social networks outside the family. Men in later life have a growing appreciation of and desire for caring relationships within the family.

> **Wife:** He had a stroke just when I thought I could lead a life of my own. I don't mean to sound selfish, but I've spent most of my life at home taking care of someone.

> **Husband**: I am devoted to my wife. She was always a good mother and wife. Taking care of her is the least I can do.

Marital Conflict

The unifying glue of marriages varies for couples. Financial security, social expectations, religious beliefs, parental demands, sexual needs, companionship needs, and personal commitment are some of the possible factors which keep couples together. All marriages, no matter how dutiful and devoted the individuals are, have sources of irritation and conflict. Older couples, as well as younger couples, become angry, laugh, and make up. Disagreements do not magically vanish in storybook fashion simply because one is old.

Some couples have grown accustomed to arguing, yet view their relationship as mutually satisfying. Parental arguing may be more difficult for adult children to accept, just as it may have been difficult when they were growing up.

> I wish Mom and Dad wouldn't fight. It's bad for Dad's blood pressure and Mom certainly doesn't need the aggravation. I used to try to smooth things over for them. I'd tell Mom how she could get Dad to stop smoking. Then I'd talk to Dad about not criticizing Mom about her weight. It doesn't make any difference what I say. I guess they'll always be like that.

2. Husbands and Wives as Caregivers

Caregiving situations can change the marital relationship significantly. The physical closeness and confinement can worsen long-standing conflicts and place an additional strain on the marital relationship. Giving and accepting care can be difficult for both spouses.

> **Wife:** Your father gets irritated at me, but I'm constantly having to remind him to take it easy. Every now and then I'll catch him making his way to the kitchen on his own. I wish he would just tell me when he needs something. I want him to get completely well. He could fall and hurt himself even worse . . . then what would I do?

> **Husband:** Your mom is constantly trying to do everything for me. You'd think I was a two-year old. She can't hear me half the time anyway when I ask for her. She won't even let me sit in bed and pay a few bills. She says she is taking care of everything. Just the thought of what the checkbook looks like is enough to send me to my grave.

The adjustments to caregiving can be awkward and uncomfortable for both husband and wife. Health limitations translate into practical changes in the division of labor, as well as qualitative changes in the relationship. Expressions of intimacy, the way in which decisions are made, how money is budgeted, and even the meaning of being together, all change. Both persons may sense a loss of personal control and increasing vulnerability.

Accepting Help

More than any other group of family caregivers, wives of dependent husbands are least likely to seek or receive support. They hesitate turning to other family members or outside resources for assistance.

> Many nights I cried myself to sleep. My only future was taking care of my husband who had irreversible brain damage. I had no idea how many months--years--it would be like that. Sometimes I wished him dead--for both our good. I was always tired. My daughter had her own family to take care of and my son was in his last year of college. What could they do?

9

I. Understanding the Situation

Spouse caregivers tend to restrict their outside social activities, even if they were once very active with other friends and family members. They are limited in part by the daily demands of caregiving, but also by their own feelings of guilt. They sometimes feel that enjoying outside activities is unfair to their frail or disabled partner.

For most older adults, accepting assistance from one's spouse is psychologically easier than accepting help from friends or family members. Social expectations of what spouses "should" do for each other in times of need encourage spouse caregiving. Although the ease with which older men and women assume these responsibilities varies, both husbands and wives generally prefer managing independently as a couple.

Social beliefs and ideals about marriage discourage spouses, particularly wives, from seeking or accepting assistance from others. "In sickness and in health, till death do us part" takes on a solitary meaning in old age when the couple tries to contain its physical, financial and emotional difficulties within the marital relationship. Pride and a desire for independence make it tough to ask for help.

Often generational boundaries within families are such that each generation tries to conceal or minimize their difficulties to other generations. It is common for adult sons and daughters to resist sharing their personal problems with their parents. It is even more characteristic of older parents to avoid bringing their problems to their children. Most older adults believe the flow of assistance should be from parent to child, the older to the younger.

In spite of tremendous financial, physical and emotional costs, parents want to avoid being a "burden" to their children and resent their children "interfering." Friends and family members may be frustrated by the older couple's refusals to accept help. In some cases, they may not realize the extent of hardships older couples face until there is a crisis.

The Loss of a Spouse

The loss of a spouse is often one of the most difficult times in a person's life. Sometimes the loss and pain are more deeply felt after the funeral. When the period of planning and condolences passes, the widowed person is left to feel the enormity of the loss alone.

Health problems and life expectancy differ for men and women, so that in most cases the wife cares for her husband. For many women, the final years of marriage are spent caring for a husband with multiple health problems. The last years together may be filled with worry, frustration, sorrow and resignation. For this reason, women in these situations have been referred to as the "hidden" victims.

The widowed person whose last few years revolved around caring for a frail spouse has lost a significant role. For some persons, caregiving gives meaning and purpose to living, only to experience a tremendous void when the husband or wife dies.

> I look at the big chair in the corner and see Bill. I look at my son and see Bill. I talk to him at breakfast. I watch television and wish he were here.

> He was so helpless when he died . . . getting up in the middle of the night to help him to the bathroom . . . changing the bedding . . . helping him shave each morning . . . helping him eat when he couldn't even hold the food in his mouth . . . as bad as it was . . . I only wish he were here.

In addition to the loss are the feelings of anger. The anger may be directed toward the spouse for having left them with all of life's burdens; toward children for having their own lives; toward friends who still have the company of their spouse; or toward oneself for not "doing more" when the person was alive.

I. Understanding the Situation

Anger, guilt, and loss are all part of the grief which follows the loss of a spouse. Widowed persons who can gradually settle within themselves their loss are better able to establish renewed interests and relationships.

The best cure for loneliness is people. Family, friends, and clergy can respect the widowed person's need to be alone, while offering an open door to emotional support. Faith and religious convictions offer many widowed persons strength. Some congregations and community groups offer widow support groups. These groups provide companionship from persons who share a common experience and better understand what each is going through.

The marital relationship is important for many older adults. The quality of older marriages can improve or deteriorate over time. In either case, caregiving is an additional strain for both spouses. Understanding the impact of caregiving is important: to avoid those areas of conflict which can be avoided and to accept those which cannot be changed.

3

SONS AND DAUGHTERS
AS CAREGIVERS

Sons and daughters often realize their parents are "getting on in years," around the same time they are increasingly aware of their own aging. For some, the realization occurs over a long period of observation and is faced with general acceptance.

> The return trip home every holiday after visiting my folks centers on how they are doing. So far we've been very fortunate. They both have their health and enough retirement income. . . . I guess we are all getting old. . . . We decided, though, that next year we should have Thanksgiving at our house. I thought they would really appreciate not having to do all the preparation . . . but I'm not sure.

For others, the reality of aging parents is a shock, often triggered by an unexpected health problem for their parents or for themselves.

> I couldn't believe it. Just last week he was bragging about his golf game. The doctor says he will have to take it easy. He may never have full use of his right arm again. We are all having to take a serious look into the future.

Increasing numbers of people in their 60s and 70s are caring for "old-old" parents who are in their 80s and 90s. As children age along with their parents, their own physical limitations increase, restricting their abilities to provide much of the physical caregiving tasks.

Becoming a Caregiver

Sons and daughters often begin their caregiving roles by checking on their parents occasionally or monitoring their overall well-being. The level of involvement may increase to 24-hour care. Adult children frequently assume primary caregiving responsibilities of one parent after the death of their other parent.

A son or daughter may become the primary caregiver for a variety of reasons. He or she may be "Dad's favorite," the "most responsible," or the one with the fewest work or family responsibilities. Sometimes it is the oldest sibling who was always the one to "take charge." Sometimes it is the youngest who "knows Mom and Dad best." Most often it is a daughter or daughter-in-law.

Family members who are divorced or never married are often expected to be the primary caregiver in the family. However, they often have fewer financial options and must struggle more with the conflict of keeping a job while managing the care of a dependent parent.

The primary caregiver may be the person who always volunteered when family members had a need:

> Sue was always there when they needed her. She would take Mom grocery shopping every Monday. She made sure Dad had his check-ups. She did laundry even when Mom didn't want her to.

Sometimes the primary caregiver is "volunteered" by other family members:

> But, Jean, you know I can't take Mom to the doctors during the week. Besides, you live much closer. And you wouldn't want her to drive herself!

In these ways and others, one family member emerges as the primary caregiver. The person is usually not chosen after considerable family thought and discussion, but rather emerges in response to family circumstances. What was thought to be a temporary situation often evolves over several years into an increasingly demanding role.

Relationship Difficulties

Some daughters and sons help their parents out of a strong affection, but others do not have a close, intimate relationship with their parents. Regardless of the level of affection, most children feel a responsibility to help. Gerontologists refer to this as "filial responsibility"--feelings of obligation or a sense of duty to one's parents.

As children become adults, they usually take on more of a peer relationship with their parents. In the mature relationship, parents and their offspring talk with each other on the level of one adult to another. In many ways, the relationship is unique. The parent and offspring interact on a mutual adult level, but they never lose sight that they **are** parent and child.

The relationship is strained when some separation between generations is not maintained. In caregiving situations, it can be difficult not to confuse the roles of parent, child and spouse.

When Dad died, Mom turned to me for help. I was divorced, living alone with my 9-year-old daughter. It made sense for her to move in with me. We could share living expenses and she would be there after school for my daughter.

It was fine in the beginning. I had wonderful images of three generations of women living together. Then Mom started needing more and more help just getting around. I was doing everything for her. After a while, I couldn't figure out who I was supposed to be. Sometimes I felt like the parent, telling Mom what she should do, and making decisions for her. And then sometimes I was a husband to her, or maybe she was my husband--or my wife--I don't know. It seemed alright at the time, but now I think we were expecting something of each other which neither of us could give.

I. Understanding the Situation

And then what really got to me was when she would treat me like a little kid again. That's when I went for counseling--just to talk with someone who could help me make sense of it all.

The shift in the relationship as one becomes an adult happens differently for individuals. It can be a gradual and relatively easy change, or it can be a difficult one. For example, an aged parent and adult offspring may maintain a dependency relationship which was appropriate in earlier years. In these situations, the older parent often becomes too involved in the affairs of the son or daughter. This situation is a problem when the parent is brought into the decision-making process which should appropriately include the adult offspring's spouse. Or the older person as grandparent may interfere in setting guidelines for grandchildren which should be set by the parents. When older members assume a psychologically powerful position, they usurp the roles of other members and potentially weaken their relationships with each other.

You would think I didn't exist. If Gloria's not over at her mom's, then she's talking to her on the phone. If Sammy has trouble in school, do you think she tells me? No! But she'll be on the horn asking her mom for advice! The other night I suggested we go to a movie. You know what she said? "But what about Mom?"

The shift in the parent-child relationship is also difficult if the adult offspring assumes too much control. When sons or daughters act as parents to their parents, the older person is stripped of an important role. Potentially, the self-worth of the older person is minimized. With good intentions, adult offspring may assume they know what is best for their parents, without considering the areas their parents may be capable of managing, or without including them in the decision-making process. This kind of control from the adult child encourages unnecessary levels of dependency. In a vulnerable state, older persons relinquish their responsibilities, in an interest to "cooperate" or to "make things easy" for the family. This creates an uncomfortable situation for both the caregiver and the care receiver.

> Eleanor takes me grocery shopping every week, which I really appreciate. But she really overdoes it. I mean, she's always fussing over me and taking care of things around the house which I would rather she left alone. I can't turn around without her doing it for me. I'm not as fast as she is, but I can still manage on my own. She means well, though, and I don't want to hurt her feelings.

Caught in the Middle

Intense parent-child bonds in later life can create added problems among other family members. The bond between an older parent and his or her offspring can weaken relationships with the offspring's own spouse and children. The expectations and needs of the different generations within older families often conflict. For this reason, adult offspring are sometimes referred to as the "sandwich generation." Caught between generations of dependent parents and dependent children, they have trouble deciding where their primary loyalties and priorities should be--to their parents, spouses or children.

Adult sons and daughters have other personal and family responsibilities. If their own children are younger and still live at home, they must look after the needs of the younger generation. If their own children are older and have left home, adult children are readjusting relationships within the family to allow for the increased independence of their children. Couples at this time of life work to establish a meaningful relationship with each other without the children occupying a large portion of their time together. Just when they are feeling a sense of relief from child rearing, they may take on responsibilities of caring for their parents.

Assessing Other Family Relationships

Family shifts in relationships take place when one person becomes closely involved with the daily care of the dependent older person. Sometimes other family members move psychologically to the sidelines and become emotionally detached from the concerns and issues of the general family. Since one member has assumed the major responsibility, they do not consider what useful role they can contribute to the welfare of the family.

Siblings and other family members can play a role in the care of older dependent members. Although the primary caregiver usually manages much of the routine care, other family members are involved in making major decisions--such as those regarding housing, medical, financial, and legal problems which arise. How the family makes decisions affects both the quality of care for the older adult and the ability of the family to give quality care.

Responding to a parent's needs may bring siblings together in a cooperative manner. Old rivalries during childhood are set aside or forgotten with the single purpose of doing the right thing for their parents. Making difficult, but joint decisions relieves the pressure from any one person and provides necessary emotional support.

> I always thought of Tom as being irresponsible. I couldn't believe he flew in from Michigan to help out when Mom got out of the hospital. He certainly has changed.
>
> ~ ~ ~ ~ ~ ~
>
> My sister was always the Miss Know-It-All, but now we talk a lot about Mom and Dad and what we can do to help. I really appreciate her asking me what I think is best. I think Mom and Dad like it, too.

Caring for parents may also resurface past sibling rivalries. Responsibilities are seldom distributed equally. Caregiving situations are ripe for inflaming resentment and jealousy. As is true in so many groups, the person who does the most is often the one who is criticized the most. Questions may arise through the family grapevine about the kind of care being given, ulterior motives for helping, or bad decisions made on behalf of the parent.

3. Sons and Daughters as Caregivers

I don't know why Sue didn't at least call us before she took Dad to that other doctor. I could have told her it was a waste of Dad's money.

The roles sons and daughters play in caring for dependent parents are complex. In responding to the needs of their parents, they must consider the needs of other family members as well as their own needs. Deciding where one's energies are best spent is difficult when the demands are great. Assessing the entire family situation and one's own limitations is a necessary step in giving appropriate and useful support to dependent parents.

4

SIBLINGS AND FRIENDS
AS SUPPORT

Traditionally, the majority of help for older adults comes from spouses and adult children. However, many older persons are single: either never-married, divorced, or widowed. Increasingly, married couples are choosing to have fewer children or no children. The declining birth rate and increasing life expectancy leave fewer younger people to care for more older people. The care of persons without spouses or children often involves other relatives and friends.

Many older adults have satisfying lives with the emotional and physical support from friends and relatives, particularly brothers and sisters. Relationships with siblings and friends do not carry the same sense of obligation as those with spouses or children. For this reason, the voluntary nature of these relationships usually makes them mutually satisfying. Siblings and friends who manage or provide primary care to an older person are usually not as emotionally involved as spouses or children. They are more likely to share the caregiving responsibilities with community health care and social service providers.

The following is a description of the support siblings and friends provide, with a look at ways they can better serve older persons. Family caregivers who are spouses or children can use this information to strengthen these potential sources of support for dependent older adults.

Siblings

Most brothers and sisters gain personal satisfaction from their relationships with each other. Siblings often draw closer after their own children are grown. Sibling relationships are especially close when they are single or childless. Re-establishing close sibling ties is meaningful in old age as individuals recall their shared family histories.

> I remember Bobby used to pick on me constantly as a kid growing up. He was a little bigger than me, you know. The only time I got the better end of the deal was when he let me win. Bobby was always the adventurous one of the pack . . . off doing his own thing. He had lots of girl friends--or so he says--but never married. Of course I was the family man. We would kid with other about how much better the other had it.

> Now that my wife is gone and Bob doesn't get around much, we've become like good buddies. We'd probably be in trouble if either of us had any steam left in us!

Most older adults have at least one brother or sister with whom they keep in contact throughout their adult years. For a few older persons, siblings are their major source of psychological support. To a smaller number of persons, siblings give them primary support in areas of social activities, financial management, and home care.

In some cases, sibling rivalry of earlier years continues into adulthood. As in all other close relationships, siblings hold differences of opinion and have disagreements. The friction may intensify when siblings must jointly work out parent-care arrangements or inheritance settlements.

Relationships between sisters are usually stronger than those between brothers. The kinds of care sisters and brothers give differs. Sisters will sometimes care for a brother if his wife dies. To a lesser extent, brothers will help a sister after the death of her husband.

4. Siblings and Friends as Support

When family support from parents or children is not available, siblings help each other in times of need. Siblings may also be potential sources of support for spouses and children who are the primary caregivers, by providing them with emotional support and respite care.

Friends

Friends are an important source of companionship for older adults. Those with close peer relationships are usually happier and less likely to become depressed for long periods of time. Friends help each other through the losses common in old age: retirement, reduced income, death of loved ones, and declining health. Emotional stability is often helped by a friend who can empathize with the older adult.

> After John died, I was in a fog for months. All of a sudden everything seemed so big and I was so small. Each day was an eternity. My children invited me over often and the grandchildren entertained me. But part of me was always somewhere else. I was empty... had nothing to give ... and couldn't accept what others wanted to give me.
>
> What helped most was being with Esther. She had lost her husband a while back. I knew she understood what I was going through the way no one else could. Whenever our husbands' names came up in conversation, there was always more than what was said. I can't put it into words. I only know that Esther and I were good friends.

Friendship bonds differ from family bonds. Friends usually share similar ages, backgrounds, and values. Unlike families, friends choose each other. That also means that individuals may end or gradually move away from friendships.

Loneliness is one of the most common problems facing older people. The loss of friendship is particularly a problem for a certain group of older adults. For example, the old-old (those over 75) have fewer friendships than the young-old. Their own physical limitations may restrict their abilities to maintain relationships through frequent visits or correspondences. Many of their friends may also be unable to maintain an ongoing relationship. Some long-standing relationships have ended in death or disability.

> I can't drive. I live alone. So what is a person my age supposed to do ? I watch a lot of television . . . and I sit here like a piece of cheese. My mistake was outliving all my friends.

Older married women who care for a frail or disabled husband often have fewer friendships. They are more likely to feel alone than are older married men. The responsibilities of managing the house, preparing meals, and caring for a frail husband leave the wife socially isolated.

Older men living alone often struggle with meeting daily needs and seeking companionship. Since women typically live longer than men, men are more likely to remarry in later life. However, the health conditions of older men are generally worse than those of older women, so that men are less socially active and have fewer new friendships. Older men are especially limited in finding other older male friends.

> I dread being around a group of old people. I'm surrounded by women! There was a time in my life when that would have been wonderful. When you're my age, it's tough finding a man to talk to.

Friends of older adults need to be aware of the reasons older persons become less involved in friendships. In many cases, it is not personal rejection but a result of their situations which draw them away from their friendships. The gradual social withdrawal of older adults may indicate a need for friends and other concerned persons to be more active in maintaining relationships.

Family members are often limited in the kind of emotional support they can give older persons. Friends outside the family can provide additional understanding and acceptance. Husbands and wives do provide emotional support; however, it is important that they maintain friendships outside their marriage. Similarly, adult children cannot provide their parents the same kinds of support their parents' same-aged friends can.

Neighborhoods, senior centers, churches, and synagogues increasingly recognize their potential to reach out to older persons. Neighbors may be the most valuable resource to older adults in emergencies because of their proximity. Older neighborhoods in established communities are especially important to older adults who have lived there for many years. An informal emergency "back-up" agreement among neighbors, like the neighborhood Crime Watch programs, can give added peace of mind to older persons and their families.

The meaning given to participation in church- and synagogue-related activities is important to many older persons. Many congregations are addressing the social and spiritual needs of its older members through a variety of programs. Some communities and congregations have collaborative Friendly Visitor programs for homebound older persons.

A small portion of older adults do not have a person on whom they can rely. These individuals are at a higher risk of institutionalization. It is through a cooperative effort among community groups that the physical, social, and emotional needs of this special group can be better addressed.

Family caregivers, including spouses and children, can strengthen the support of an older adult by drawing on other relationships both inside and outside the family. The care given by one person should not exclude the care given by others. Rather, each person should supplement or complement the care given by others. The exercise titled

I. Understanding the Situation

"Circles of Support" on page 36 helps caregivers realize potential sources of support beyond the immediate family.

In younger years, friends outside the family are usually easily made through numerous social contacts: school, work, social activities. In later life, caregivers and older adults are more limited in their ability to maintain friendships. Siblings and friends are valuable sources of support for both primary caregivers and dependent older persons. They can reduce the stress of caregiving and improve the general well-being of the older person.

5

THE "SUPER" CAREGIVER

"Super" caregivers are those who are so invested in the life of the dependent person that they lose sight of their own separate identities. They take on the problems of the older person with more emotional investment than they would if the problems were their own. Unfortunately, many caregivers feel this is the appropriate way to respond to the needs of dependent family members. Although the intent is to help, this pattern of help can be destructive for everyone.

Knowing when to Intervene

Many people have great difficulty separating their personal feelings and problems from those of others, especially those of loved ones. In becoming involved in the affairs of others, family members risk taking over in areas which should appropriately be left for the other person to handle.

Mom used to complain to me that her other children didn't visit her enough in the nursing home. It was really a problem between my mom and my brothers, but I, of course, tried to fix it for her. So I complained to my brothers about their not visiting more. And I visited Mom every day for six months straight to sort of make up for my brothers' not being around and to make them feel guilty. A lot of good that did!

Other times when Mom was mad about something, I would be there to try to make it right for her, but rarely could. It took a long time before I realized that the most I could do was let her know I understood her ailments and complaints. All the worry in the world wouldn't change her situation. My getting upset every time she got upset did neither of us any good.

I. Understanding the Situation

Primary caregivers may become anxious or upset over issues which present no problem for others. People differ in their perceptions and responses of situations. What one person thinks is serious is not a serious matter for another. Family members--young and old--live by different priorities, values, and expectations. In showing their concern for older persons, caregivers may identify problems which are of little concern to the older person.

Knowing just when to intervene in the affairs of older relatives is difficult. In general, older adults should maintain control over matters of personal opinion. However, caregivers may decide to intervene in serious life-threatening situations which may not be taken seriously by the older adult.

> If you see a maroon car with no driver, that's my mother-in-law. She can barely see over the steering wheel. She has had three tickets for running stop signs in the last three months. No telling how many she has run and not been caught. Something has got to be done about it.

Frail or disabled older adults need to control decisions affecting their own lives as much as possible. Understanding the older person's need for both dependence and independence is one of the most difficult issues caregivers face. An inaccurate assessment results in offering either too little or too much support. If the older person's dependency needs are not heard, the caregiver may fail to give the necessary encouragement and support. Yet, in overreacting to the dependency needs, the caregiver may offer premature solutions when the needs demand the older person's personal resolution.

Caregiving as a Family Role

Super caregivers may feel responsible in some way for everyone in the family. Sometimes they become overly protective, taking it upon themselves to monitor unnecessarily the personal well-being of others. Most likely it is the family role with which the caregiver is most familiar. It is difficult sharing the responsibilities of caregiving when it is central to one's self-identity and when other family members have not shared the responsibilities in the past.

> My mom called last night. She told me about all she is doing for my grandparents now. She gets off work early on Fridays and drives home to make supper for my brother. (He's 26 years old and still lives at home. Mom does all his washing and cooking.)
>
> She drives to my grandparents' house, an hour away, to take Grandaddy to the doctor's and Grandmother to the health food store downtown. (Mom hates driving downtown!) Mom buys groceries for them and stays up late cleaning their house.
>
> My mother worries about them constantly. Grandaddy talks to her about how she has got to take care of Grandmother when he dies. Grandmother's always complaining to her about Grandaddy's bathroom habits, expecting Mom to make him "clean up his act."
>
> On top of all this, she will pick up my sister's two kids and keep them over the weekend. My sister has a crummy marriage, so Mom thinks if she and her husband just had time together, maybe things would be alright between them.
>
> I don't know what we would do without Mom!

Most families encourage the overextended caregiver with praise and sympathy. Family roles like "Poor Mom" or "Super Sis" become part of the caregiver identity. These family roles are self-perpetuating and are difficult to break.

When Helping Hurts

Unfortunately, such intensive levels of involvement can be detrimental to the caregiver, the care-receiver, and other family members. When primary caregivers assume unrealistic levels of responsibility, they intensify their own suffering, often unnecessarily. The more involved a single family member is, the less involved other family members become.

I. Understanding the Situation

Dependent older persons in the hands of super caregivers have their physical needs met, but sometimes at the expense of their own sense of autonomy and self-worth. Overinvolved primary caregivers also lose their own sense of autonomy. Their excessive concern inhibits effective problem solving, particularly in times of stress, either by overreacting or by being immobilized by the severity. When resentment builds over time, the quality of care declines.

Unfortunately, other family members may not recognize the primary caregiver's need for support. In an attempt to appear to be managing independently, caregivers avoid asking for assistance. They may try to keep the family running smoothly by absorbing the pressures themselves and by not asking too much of others. It is often not until the primary caregiver or the dependent older person has a major physical setback that other family members are made aware of the need for their assistance. When a crisis does occur, the entire family usually makes shifts to accommodate the immediate circumstances.

> After six months of taking care of my grandparents, on top of the pressures of her job, Mom ended up in the hospital. The doctor said her intestinal and bladder problems were probably brought on by stress. It's awful to say, but we all knew Mom was doing too much. It wasn't until she collapsed that we were able to help her.

The following chapters look at setting realistic expectations and alternative ways of responding to others in need. Caregivers must learn to separate their own feelings and needs from those of the dependent person. Then they can better cope with problem situations inherent in any helping relationship.

Two exercises which deal with expectations and feelings are included in the activities accompanying Part I. "Through the Eyes of Others" on page 34 helps caregivers identify possible ways in which they are living up to others' expectations. The "Feelings Checklist" on page 38 examines both positive and negative feelings which often accompany caregiving.

ACTIVITIES

UNDERSTANDING THE SITUATION

o Situation Inventory

o Lifestyle Changes

o Through the Eyes of Others

o Circles of Support

o Caregiver's Feelings Checklist

SITUATION INVENTORY

1. How is the person for whom you care related to you?
   (Example: mother, husband, father-in law)

2. Family members become the primary caregiver of a frail or disabled older person for a variety of reasons. How did you become a caregiver ?

3. What are the physical and mental limitations of your older relative ?

4. Check the kinds of assistance you currently give.

____	Telephone regularly	____	Home repair, yardwork
____	Prepare meals	____	Manage finances
____	Housework, cleaning, laundry	____	Personal care (dressing, bath, etc.)
____	Nursing care (bed care, shots, etc.)	____	Provide transportation to visit friends and relatives
____	Transportation to religious services, social and recreational activities	____	Transportation to shopping, medical, banking, and other business services
____	Other: _____		

5. To what extent are you worried about the kind of care your older relative needs now or may need in the future ?

   Some _____   Considerable _____   Very much _____

LIFESTYLE CHANGES

Sometimes helping others takes considerable time and energy. In what ways is your life affected by your caring for an older family member? Please briefly describe the adjustment(s) or change(s) you have made.

____ Work:

____ Social life:

____ Leisure, recreation , vacation:

____ Education:

____ Finances:

____ Health, exercise, diet:

____ Spiritual life:

____ Family relationships (with spouse, children, siblings, etc.):

What realistic lifestyle changes could you make to improve the quality of life for yourself and your older relative ?

THROUGH THE EYES OF OTHERS

The way significant people in our lives see us affects how we view ourselves and how we respond to situations.

1. In the boxes on the opposite page write: (1) how each significant person in your life would describe you; (2) what each person expects of you?

2. Which roles/descriptions do you like?

3. Which descriptions would you like to change?

4. What might you realistically do to begin making desired changes in your relationships with significant persons in your life?

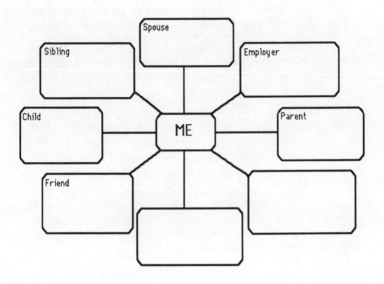

I. Understanding the Situation

CIRCLES OF SUPPORT

Sometimes it is difficult to recognize potential sources of support for dependent older relatives. The purpose of this exercise is to identify current or potential sources of support for you and your older family member.

Step 1. On the next page are 4 circles:

1. In the inner circle place the name of your older relative.
2. In the second circle write the names or initials of those persons who are currently providing ongoing assistance to you or your older relative.
3. In the third circle, indicate the persons who look after the older person in a limited way. Persons may include neighbors, friends, and relatives.
4. In the outer circle, persons who are not currently involved but who could be asked.

Step 2.

1. How comfortable are you with the number of available support persons?

Uncomfortable   Comfortable
1 - 2 - 3 - 4 - 5

2. Are you using your support network to the fullest extent you need?
Yes _____ No _____

3. If you are underutilizing your support network, what is keeping you from it? (Example: beliefs, attititudes, concerns)

4. In what ways could you encourage improvement in the quantity and quality of support you and your relative receive?

Person	How They Help Now	(Realistic) Helpful Changes

36

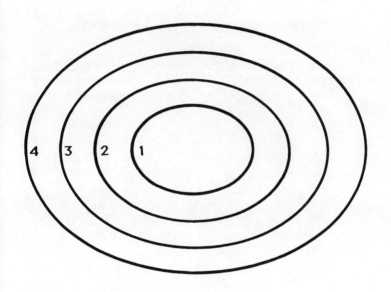

CAREGIVER'S FEELINGS CHECKLIST

Family members often have both positive and negative feelings. These feelings emerge from situations involving a dependent older person, other family members, friends and outside groups such as social service and health care agencies.

Please check those feelings you have recently experienced and briefly explain their source.

Feeling	**Explanation**

Example:

___√___ Thankfulness	*For the many years of being together*
___√___ Anger	*That others in the family don't do more*
_____ Love	
_____ Helplessness	
_____ Embarrassment	
_____ Concern	
_____ Hope	
_____ Guilt	
_____ Empathy	
_____ Loneliness	
_____ Depression	

Other feelings:

II

UNDERSTANDING RELATIONSHIPS

By now it is apparent that one family member will usually take on the primary caregiving responsibilities. Yet, how much is realistic for one person to do? What is the role of other family members? How can the caregiving tasks and decisions be shared? How can caregivers communicate their own needs? How can caregivers best handle problems of other family members?

This part addresses these important questions. Chapter 6 looks at the limitations primary caregivers face. Chapter 7 explains the importance of interdependence and reciprocity both within the family and the community at large. Chapters 8 and 9 give practical guidelines for improving the communication in older families. Finally, Chapter 10 encourages the involvement of all family members in the caregiving tasks and decision making.

6

ACCEPTING LIMITATIONS

Dealing effectively with the problems inherent in caregiving begins with acceptance. First, caregivers must accept their own physical and emotional needs. They are not solely responsible for relationships within the family. Nor can they do all and be all for dependent family members.

Second, caregivers must accept the older person, for whatever he or she was or was not. The injustices in the relationship from the past can be a tremendous burden if carried into the present caregiving relationship. Older adults should neither be set on a pedestal nor cast aside for their increased dependency needs.

Accepting Personal Limitations

Most caregivers start with the noblest of intentions--and an unrealistic picture of the situation they face. Initially, they believe that with a little effort, they can make it all right again. Then they discover that the situations may get worse. Over time, they realize that the demands are becoming greater. They become easily frustrated, and short-tempered. Then they feel guilty for not being more patient and more giving.

> I was so mad at her because she kept asking me to get her this and get her that. So I told her that was it. From then on she could get her own stuff. I had no idea she would try walking down to the basement. . . . If only I had been there when she fell.

Primary caregivers are often viewed by others as the hub of the family. As a central figure in the family, they may assume the impossible task of making everyone in the family get along.

> Mother was 62 when she moved in with Fred and me. Things were fine the first few years. Then Fred had his operation and was home for six months recuperating. It was all I could do to keep them from killing each other. Mother would do ornery things like put a load of clothes on just when Fred was about to take a shower, knowing full well he wouldn't have any hot water. I was constantly keeping peace between them.

How family members choose to relate to each other is their shared responsibility. It is not the responsibility of the caregiver. Family peacemakers set themselves up for disappointment as well as personal attack.

> Dad's health is failing rapidly. He has been in the hospital for 3 weeks now. And we honestly don't know if he will live much longer. They have him hooked up to all sorts of equipment.
>
> It has been really tough on Mom. It would be much easier for Mom if only my brother, Bill, would visit. He and Dad never did get along in spite of Mom's best efforts to get them on speaking terms.
>
> So I thought I would see what I could do. I wrote Bill a long letter and told him all about Dad and how it would help if he would at least call. When I showed the letter to Mom, she got mad and told me to leave him alone. . . . I don't understand it.

As painful as it may be for the primary caregiver, family members take responsibility for their own relationships.

Making family members happy is another unrealistic goal. Statements such as "I only want to make her happy" presume that a person can control how another feels. Similarly, "If only" statements, such as "If only I could visit more," presume that happiness is completely dependent on external circumstances and can be manipulated by changing the circumstances. In caregiving situations, the health conditions of the older person may improve, but even if all illness and pain disappeared, it would not guarantee "happiness."

6. Accepting Limitations

It is difficult to handle the daily frustrations of dealing with someone else's physical handicaps. For example, hearing impairment, vision loss, arthritis, and incontinence can tax the patience of anyone over time. Most difficult to accept are the memory loss and disorientation which accompany Alzheimer's disease or other forms of dementia.

> I knew she can't help herself . . . but do you know what it's like telling someone for the tenth time where you just came from? Or telling your **own** mother what your name is? Or pretending like you're listening to those ridiculous, rambling stories.
>
> For a while I can take it. But then, I'll get angry . . . even though I know she can't help it. Sometimes I'll just ignore her questions and pretend she's not there.

Many caregivers confront their own emotional limitations to love. The modern romanticized ideal of "love" rarely fits the caregiving situation. Feelings of affection change over time. Feelings for a newborn baby, a teenage son, or one's aged parents may carry similar concerns for their well-being, but do not carry the same emotional closeness or strong affection. The "I-can't-live-without-you" sentiment expressed in popular "love" songs does not describe the sentiment found in most caregiving relationships. Caregivers who accept the popular sentimental version of what family relationships "should" be, feel guilty when their own experience is less than the ideal.

Caught in an emotional bind, caregivers may ask themselves: "Can I care for a person I do not love?" The answer is yes. A genuine, caring concern for a person may be motivated by a sense of responsibility, rather than a close affection for the person. An intense affection is not necessary for effective caregiving.

In fact, caregivers who have the strongest feelings of closeness and affection for the dependent older person, sometimes have the greatest burden. Affection and burden can work against each other, creating emotional confusion and

43

making the caregiver less effective in coping with difficult situations.

Accepting the Older Person

Accepting limitations includes accepting the older person's dependency. Health problems may leave a person physically demanding and unattractive. It can be difficult to love and care for a person who is extremely dependent.

Accepting the limitations of the older person also includes forgiving them for not being more than they were. The caregiver who cannot let go of past hurts continues to suffer emotional pain. Care is given grudgingly when past resentments persist.

> I wanted so much to love my father, to let him know everything was okay. But I just looked at him lying there and I couldn't help remembering all the times he hurt Mom. Life was always one big joke to him and I wasn't about to take him seriously--not even then. I'll do what I can to help him stay alive, but don't expect any more from me.

Stress within families is greater when their goals are not realistic or achievable. Primary caregivers sometimes have difficulty accepting the limitations of the dependent person and other family members. They often have difficulty accepting their own physical and emotional limitations.

Caregivers who have trouble either accepting their own limitations or the limitations of the older person can benefit from open discussion with a caring concerned person. Such a person might be a member of the clergy, a counselor, family therapist, or other professional resource person.

7

INTERDEPENDENCE
AND RECIPROCITY

Western culture emphasizes independence as the ideal, as exemplified in expressions like "rugged individualism" and "self-determination." The reality is that none of us are independent. Each person--young and old, weak and strong--benefits and contributes to the whole.

Understanding Interdependence

The concept of interdependence requires that family members give and accept assistance as needed, while respecting the need to engage in private, independent activities. We let family members know in subtle ways that we respect their individuality, yet are willing to help them when they need and want it. The expression of interdependence is found in the ways family members communicate.

Most people prefer being the "helper" as opposed to being the one "helped." People will often take care of others and encourage them to live healthy lifestyles, while abusing themselves with poor diets, lack of exercise and only emergency physical examinations. All people generally want to feel useful to others. We need to be needed.

Caregivers can use this information about the basic human desire to be needed in two ways: First, the way in which the caregiver accepts help serves as an important model for family members of all ages. It may be easier for older adults to accept more dependent relationships when caregivers understand and accept their own dependency needs.

Second, in dealing with older adults who are increasingly dependent, it is important to let them know in specific ways how they are helpful. Statements of appreciation are important in any relationship, but particularly in helping relationships. For example, the caregiver may frequently need to ask the older person to change a certain behavior or do a favor. The response of the older person will vary depending on how the request is presented. Requests that begin with, "It would help me. . ." are more positively received, than orders ("You must. . ."), or threats ("If you don't. . ."). Rather than feeling belittled or inferior, the older person is put in a position of giving. Simple changes in communication can make a dependent relationship more acceptable to both persons.

Giving and Receiving

We tend to think of giving and receiving in concrete, tangible terms such as giving services; or in materialistic terms such as giving a present. Expressions such as "one good turn deserves another" and "I owe you one" remind us that when someone does us a favor, we want to "repay" within a relatively short time.

These beliefs about giving and how to give in return are difficult to apply to the exchanges among family members. Both the giving and receiving are difficult when an immediate tangible or materialistic exchange cannot be given or accepted. Relationships are strained when one person feels he or she is giving more than receiving. Sometimes a long history of felt injustices surface under the pressures of caregiving.

> I did everything for Harry--raised his kids, washed his clothes, picked up his underwear, even while knowing he was running around on me. I never said one word. 47 years! And now I'm supposed to do

everything for him--even walk him to the bathroom. Sometimes he'll
ask me to hold his hand or kiss him. I'll do anything else, but not
that. . . . He has hurt me too much.

The entire exchange process can become awkward in
older families. Adult children may be uncomfortable receiving
gifts from older parents, knowing their parents are in need
themselves. Adult children may also need to prove their own
independence by not accepting assistance from parents.

Similarly, older parents may not readily accept gifts of
goods or services from their children. Parents may feel that
grown children can better spend their time and money on their
own personal needs. The position and self-worth of older
parents may be threatened by their children's increasing
resources from which to give and their own decreasing
resources. They may strongly believe that the older
generation should always be the "giver." Or as one older
person remarked about his children bringing him "goodies," "I
don't need the junk!"

However, parents, children, grandparents, friends, and
neighbors give, not merely because the other person is in
need, but because they need to give.

Understanding Reciprocity

There are ways of looking at social exchanges which can
help both the caregiver and care receiver in older families
accept the inherent inequities in their situations:

First, the reciprocity of giving and receiving need not occur
within a short time period, but can be viewed across the life
span. In this way, care is accepted in old age for the care
given in earlier years.

Mom has had three different operations in the past year. She cared
for me when I was young, so I now take care of her. It's that simple.

47

II. Understanding Relationships

Caregivers must take caution to balance their sense of reciprocity with realistic expectations. Giving care willingly out of appreciation for care received earlier can create problems if taken to an extreme. For example, many family members feel guilty when they are not able to cope with the emotional, physical, and financial burdens. Reciprocity must be balanced with realistic expectations. Unrealistic expectations result in guilt and ill-feelings.

Second, giving must not be limited to tangible or materialistic goods and services. Giving also includes intangibles such as an idea, a sense of history, a purpose, a suggestion, an understanding of self. It is important that dependent persons are valued for the intangibles they contribute to others.

> It hasn't been easy taking care of my wife the last eight years, but we do the best we can. The children know a part about life they wouldn't know otherwise. Their mom has given the family an excuse to be together. She has been a good example for all of us and I tell her so whenever I think she's able to understand what I'm saying.

Finally, reciprocity does not need to be confined to two persons, but can be shared among several people. For example, parents may give to their children in return for what their parents gave them. Adult children may care for their parents in return for the future care their children may give them in old age.

When reciprocal exchanges are not possible between two people, they can be viewed within the larger society--not only within families, but also within workplaces, congregations, and neighborhoods. A sense of community reciprocity and inter-dependence can be difficult for individuals to accept and apply. The strength of community interdependence is that it does not limit caregiver support to blood-related family members.

7. Interdependence and Reciprocity

Last winter Mr. Johnson, our next door neighbor, had a second aneurysm operation. Mrs. Johnson didn't drive so we took her to the hospital every afternoon. Their son lives in Washington and their daughter lives 45 minutes away. I know the family appreciated our helping. I suspect the day will come when my parents in Virginia will need help and a neighbor or friend will help them when I can't.

Principles of interdependence and reciprocity can guide primary caregivers of frail or disabled older adults. Families can better serve their older members by understanding the human desire for comparable exchanges of giving and receiving. Caregivers can help older persons accept help by modeling their own acceptance of help from others in the community. Families, congregations, businesses, communities, and countries are more effective in responding to the needs of others when they understand how each person--young and old, weak and strong--contributes to the whole.

8

CARING ENOUGH
TO LISTEN

People communicate not only to relay information but also to define relationships. How family members communicate affects the quality of the relationship as well as the degree of understanding.

Individuals usually have conflicting feelings at any given time, so one might be simultaneously happy about one thing and sad about something else. The feelings among older adults and other family members may include thankfulness and love, as well as anger, guilt and sorrow. A person may also feel "down," yet not know why. Having someone to talk to can help sort out the feelings.

People who are experiencing intense negative emotions have trouble making rational decisions. It is difficult to make decisions when one is fuming with anger, overwhelmed with sorrow, or anxious about the future. Suppressed feelings worsen problems and discourage clear thinking.

Listening is the most effective response to persons who are experiencing problems. Listening and hearing are not the same. Assuming no physiological impairment, hearing is an ordinary occurrence. Listening, however, is a more complex and difficult process. Listening means recognizing and acknowledging the **meaning** of what a person says.

Nonverbal Communication

We communicate our basic attitudes and feelings mostly nonverbally. **What** we say is not as important as **how** we say it.

II. Understanding Relationships

Eye contact and facial expressions show how interested or uneasy one is. Voice tone and volume can be fast and unpleasant or slow, clear, and comforting. Standing far apart inhibits communication, while standing too close can be intrusive or threatening. Touch can show support and care, or it can show control and manipulation.

Touching is one of the most effective ways of expressing care. Unfortunately, older adults are not touched in kind ways as much as are younger persons. In our society, touching wrinkled skin is not encouraged. Families also differ in how comfortable they are in showing physical expressions of affection. Hugging, holding, or gently touching can be especially difficult for men showing affection to other male family members.

Caregivers can avoid the pressure of having the "right" thing to say by saying it all with a touch. Holding an older person's hand or shoulder, even without an exchange of words, can be a powerful way to communicate caring and comfort.

These are all important aspects of communication to remember in caregiving. It is easy to be consumed with the daily tasks of caregiving and forget about the subtle but powerful messages sent by a brief pause in the routine, a touch, and a gentle smile.

Sometimes we send conflicting nonverbal and verbal messages. The caregiver who grits her teeth and says, "Oh, I don't mind" is not being honest to herself or the other person.

I could always tell when Grandmother and Mom were mad at each other. Grandmother would be sitting alone in her bedroom with the television blaring and Mom would be running the vacuum cleaner like crazy outside her door. That was my cue to disappear fast.

When there is a discrepancy in the person's nonverbal and verbal message, it is the nonverbal which is the more honest.

8. Caring Enough to Listen

Caregivers need to be aware of the nonverbal messages they are sending, as well as the nonverbal messages they receive. They may be able to identify feelings and needs which the older adult has not been able to put into words.

Some Dos and Don'ts of Listening

Communicating with persons who have strong needs is difficult. Primary caregivers are often in situations of having to respond to family members who bring their problems to them. Unfortunately, some of our most common ways of responding to others are not helpful and may even be destructive to the older person, the caregiver, and to their relationship.

Descriptions and examples of responses which are less helpful are discussed below. Samples of more helpful responses are also given.

1. Helpful listening does **not** mean making the older person "feel better" by talking about someone else who has similar or worse problems. When people are uncomfortable hearing about someone's problems, or when their own needs are great, they will often try to change the subject. This distracts from the other person, who is not allowed to express his concerns.

Family Member:	"You can't imagine how painful it has been."
Unhelpful Response:	Interrupting or withdrawal
	"You think you've got problems, let me tell you. . . . Anyway, let's not talk about that now."
Helpful Response:	"Tell me about it."

53

2.   Helpful listening does **not** mean preventing the person from talking about negative feelings of anger, grief, or depression by reassuring or praising them.

We use reassurance to let another person know things will get better. Sometimes the distressed person may not be ready to hear comforting or reassuring words. Other times, the circumstances are such that reassuring comments are unrealistic and inappropriate. Most importantly, reassurance may be interpreted as discounting the person's feelings or suggesting that his problems are insignificant.

Similarly, complimenting or praising a person for their abilities or accomplishments is intended to be encouraging. However, when a distressed person receives praise, it can set unrealistic expectations or standards. It can also be controlling and manipulative. Compliments should be given when the person is **not** emotionally upset.

Family Member:	"I don't think I can manage much longer."
Unhelpful Response:	Reassuring
	"Now, now. Just think about the good side of things. It will be better in no time."
Unhelpful Response:	Praising beyond circumstantial facts
	"You're a fighter if there ever was one. You always come through in the end, no matter what."
Helpful Response:	"It's been pretty tough on you, hasn't it."

3. Helpful listening does **not** mean giving advice. Whenever possible, persons who are most affected by a problem should have a major role in the decision-making process. Giving suggestions or solutions discourages a sense of competence and control. It tends to communicate a position

of superiority and a lack of confidence in the other person's judgment.   This is particularly a problem for older adults who are increasingly dependent.

Sometimes advice includes messages of criticism.   This adds to a person's feelings of inferiority or defensiveness. People defensively   reject even good advice and accurate criticism in order to protect their own self-image.   Thus, giving advice can have the opposite effect from what is desired.

Finally, giving advice puts undue pressure on the caregiver to have the "right" answers.   The solutions the caregiver has may not be right for the other person or simply may not work. So many problems in life do not have right answers.   As much as possible, no one family member should have the burden of making right decisions.

Family Member:	"I don't know what to do."
Unhelpful Response:	Giving advice
	"If I were you, I would. . . . " " Why don't you just. . . ?"
Unhelpful Response:	Moralizing or judging
	"You should have thought about this a long time ago."
Helpful Response:	Affirming the difficulty and encouraging problem-solving
	"It sounds like a really tough situation. What are some of your alternatives?"

The most common communication mistakes people make when talking with someone who has a problem are: (1) interruption and avoidance; (2) reassurance and praise; and (3) judging and advice giving. A simpler response of reflective listening is more effective in communicating understanding and acceptance.

Reflective Listening

Family and friends help most by listening to the feeling underlying what is said. Much of what we want to communicate is unclear, hidden or distorted. Often, what is said may not be what is intended or heard.

Family caregivers can actively listen, by reflecting back what they heard. They can increase understanding in the relationship and encourage effective problem solving by clarifying the communication.

For example, an older adult might ask in a concerned voice, "Would you please go with me to the doctor's?" By listening to both the verbal and nonverbal cues, the caregiver might think that the person is worried or afraid about going. The caregiver could reflect back what he heard by saying, "You sound a bit worried and might want someone to be there with you?" If the feedback is accurate and confirmed by the older person, the door is open for the person to express any concerns.

Older Adult: "Would you go with me to the doctors?"

Caregiver: "You seem a little worried about it?"

Older Adult: "Yes, I get the results from the lab test. It could be serious."

Conversely, if the listener finds that the feedback is incorrect, then the speaker can clarify the message. By reflecting back to the person, possible misunderstandings and conflict are avoided. Often the person will not only clarify their position, but open new lines of communication.

Older Adult: "No, I'm not worried. It would just be nice to have you along. . . . I have lost my keys though. Have you seen them?

56

When helpful listening responses are used, several positive results occur. The conversation focuses on the needs of the person. The person with the problem feels understood and accepted. Problem solving is encouraged without the listener taking over.

It is difficult to "just" listen when one is accustomed to other response patterns. The exercise titled "Listening with Care" on page 77 encourages caregivers to set aside short periods of time to listen. With practice, reflective listening becomes a more natural and effective communication skill.

Special Considerations

Communicating with persons who have certain physical or mental difficulties requires special attention. Hearing loss, aphasia or mental disorientation can increase the social isolation of older adults. Caregivers need to consult health professionals for suggestions on the specific needs of the older individual. Under these special circumstances, the following communciation principles are especially helpful:

1. Establish eye contact.

2. Include more nonverbal messages such as head nodding and pointing to objects.

3. Use short sentences.

4. Speak clearly, without over enunciating.

As much as possible, older adults should be included in discussions. The family should not talk about the older person in his presence, even if the person shows no indication of comprehension. In all cases, the older person should be regarded as a communicating individual, even though he or she may not understand what is said.

Talking about Death

Most families avoid talking about death. Yet silence can deprive necessary comfort and support to those about to die and to those who care for them. The reality of death can be difficult for family members. Understanding one's own concerns is important to the process of comforting others.

We often try to "cheer up" a person in serious distress, or we busy ourselves with activity--anything to avoid talking about the fears of death. Responses such as "Don't talk like that" or "Come now, you'll outlive all of us" are usually not helpful. Such messages imply that the dying person "shouldn't think like that." The person is left feeling not understood, alone, and hopeless. A simple "I understand" or a nonverbal acknowledgment of the difficulties can convey the necessary acceptance and support.

Listening to stories and remembrances of past experiences helps. An informal review of one's life occurs while looking at family photographs, old newspapers, and magazine clippings. Recalling both the good and bad times allows the older person to put the past into perspective, to accept the accomplishments and failures. Good listeners encourage life reviews.

Thoughts and feelings about death vary. Different religious beliefs and the meaning given to death must be accepted as reality for the dying person and not be debated. Caring persons can take their cues from the person regarding what he or she wants to talk about. While some want to avoid the subject of death, most persons are relieved and grateful to have an opportunity to express their feelings. Terminally ill persons and their close friends and family often go through different emotions, including denial, anger, bargaining, depression, and acceptance. Caregivers can be sensitive to the changing emotions which accompany increasing dependency and impending death.

8. Caring Enough to Listen

The physical and emotional stress for family members is particularly trying during prolonged terminally ill conditions. The primary caregiver may become irritable or angry, and then feel guilty about not being more patient and consoling. Accepting one's own feelings and limitations makes it easier.

During difficult times, caregivers may not be able to make bad times good. They can, however, work to ease the pain by listening and accepting the difficult realities of life.

9

CARING ENOUGH
TO CONFRONT

Primary caregivers have a responsibility to themselves and to their families to seek solutions to caregiving problems. These solutions should minimize the stress for any one family member. The quality of care given to the dependent person is better if the physical and emotional needs of the primary caregiver are also addressed. In other words, caregivers must take care of themselves in order to take care of others.

Expressing Feelings

Feelings toward a dependent person may include not only love, empathy, and compassion, but also guilt, resentment, frustration, anxiety, and hostility. For many, the negative feelings are personally unacceptable. Caregivers may try to cover "bad" feelings with false pretenses that "everything is okay."

Unfortunately, when concerns are not addressed, they build over time, then emerge in destructive ways. Days, months, and even years of annoyances are sometimes stored, only to be released in the form of anger or depression.

> I was tired of yelling all the time so we bought him a hearing aid. But he refused to wear it. I don't know what came over me. He had the television turned up so loud I couldn't hear myself think, and the hearing aid was just sitting there on the coffee table. . . . I turned off the TV, picked up the hearing aid, and threw it across the room and just started yelling at him. I could tell he was shocked and hurt.

> After I calmed down and apologized, we were able to talk about it. He had no idea his not wearing the hearing aid was a problem for me.

Sometimes unexpressed negative feelings toward one person are directed at other persons in the family.

> My mother-in-law moved in "temporarily" six months ago. She quickly settled in and made herself "useful." She started giving me pointers on how to cook. She complained about the dust in the house and rearranged the cabinets and my plants, so "everything looked neater." I couldn't believe it. I was **living** all those mother-in-law jokes. Only it wasn't funny.

> I wanted her to feel at home, so of course I didn't say anything which would hurt her feelings. But the tension in the house is incredible now. We are all smiles around Grandmother, but Dick and I are arguing every chance we get. I am constantly nagging the kids to do more around the house and to spend more time with their grandmother. The more I nag, the more they hole up in their rooms.

Caregivers owe it to themselves and others in the family to be honest about their concerns and needs. Even "insignificant" nuisances can seriously affect critical aspects of caring relationships.

Saying No

Caregivers need to be able to say no to excessive, inappropriate or unrealistic demands. The person in the family who takes on the caregiving role is often the one who is quickest to say "I'll do it." The more commitments and promises made, the less likely the caregiver is to fulfill obligations. Then, broken promises often lead to other promises which cannot be met, only to add to the guilt and ill feelings.

> I promised Dad I would take care of Mom when he died. . . . "She would always have a place in our home," I said. He was counting on me to look after her.

I felt awful when I put Mom in the nursing home. I really had to. But I promised Mom when we took her to the nursing home that I would visit her every day . . . and I haven't missed a day yet. . . .

Requests from children, spouses, parents, and siblings do not demand automatic yes responses. Primary caregivers are limited in what they can realistically manage. The overload of tasks becomes critical for the family when one person assumes a disproportionate share of responsibilities. Such inequitable arrangements breed later resentment.

Accepting Help

Although the physical and emotional demands of caregiving can be high, caregivers are often reluctant to ask for help from friends, neighbors, and other family members. It is difficult for caregivers to give themselves permission to take care of their own needs. They sometimes view their need for help as a negative reflection of their inability to "provide for their own"--as a failure to live up to their own unrealistic standards of caring.

Family caregivers must take partial responsibility if they feel overburdened and have not sought assistance. People often assume others know or "should" know what they need. Unfortunately, family members, friends, and neighbors often do not understand the caregiver's needs unless they are explicitly stated.

John and Louise kept Mom for over two years before John said anything to me about how hard it was for him and his wife. I figured they probably had some tough moments, but that things were generally okay. I had no idea what they were going through until he wrote me a letter. He could have just told me. I was glad to help out.

Ending Blame

A normal, but ineffective, response to problems is deciding whose fault it is. Children blame parents; parents blame children. Husbands blame wives; wives blame husbands. Old people blame themselves; caregivers blame themselves.

Blaming remarks often begin with "You made me . . .", "If it weren't for you. . .", "Why don't you . . .", "You're always . . . ", "If only I had . . ." Such statements tend to **end**, rather than **extend** constructive conversations. Blaming messages only lead to resistance and resentment.

Sometimes older persons who are sensitive about their increased dependency blame themselves for family problems, even though family members do not fault them. In other cases, marital conflict and parent-child conflict are falsely attributed to the demands placed on the family by the needs of the older member. Eventually, others in the family begin viewing the older person as the problem without regard to other sources of stress in the family.

> If only Grandmother were not around, then Mom and Dad wouldn't have to argue so much.

Family members may also use primary caregivers as scapegoats for their problems. Since it is easier to find fault with the person doing the most, caregivers are likely candidates for blame. Older persons may take out their frustrations of being dependent on the caregiver, by being overly demanding or critical. They may show more affection or higher regard to other relatives and discount the importance of the assistance given by the primary caregiver.

The caregiver may blame other family members for not being more attentive to the older person's needs. They may do more to compensate for the others' underinvolvement. The more they do, the more they fault others.

Guidelines for Confronting

The difficult nature of caregiving situations demands that caregivers clearly communicate their problems. They may need to confront government bureaucracies or hospital personnel on behalf of an older person. They may need to confront other family members to resolve critical issues of care. They may need to confront the dependent person on routine daily matters and on major life decisions.

The following are some principles to follow for effective confrontation:

1. **Effective confrontation includes listening.** People listen to those who first hear them. If a confrontation is to be heard and accepted, the caregiver must be ready to listen carefully to the other person.

2. **The time and setting should be comfortable for the other person.** The fewer distractions there are, the more likely the confrontation will lead to better understanding and resolution.

3. **Each person must speak for himself or herself.** Statements which begin with "I think . . .", "I feel . . .", and "I need . . ." are more likely to be honest expressions of one's perceptions. Statements beginning with "You said . . .," "We think . . .", "They mean . . ." speak for other people. Such comments can be misleading, evasive, and manipulative.

4. Effective confronting statements **focus on the behavior, not on the person.** Clear, nonjudgmental statements of actions increase understanding and invite helpful change. Character attacks do not solve problems.

5. **The description of the problem should be stated in neutral, non-evaluative language** to avoid defensive responses. Words like "never," "always," "all," and "none" generally cause the discussion to focus on the **extent** of the problem rather than the resolution of the problem.

6. **Explore ideas and options together.** Solutions which are worked out together and are mutually agreed upon are

more successful than solutions which are dictated by one person.

7. **Express frustrations, irritations, hurts, and fears without anger.** Anger is often an explosion of negative feelings accumulated over time. Angry confrontations usually leave the other person feeling threatened. Their normal reaction is to flee or fight back. Anger does not promote cooperative problem-solving.

8. Finally, **be positive, persistent, and patient.** Change takes time.

Open communication is important to families. Effective listening and confronting ease the burden for families as they face the difficulties of caring for frail or disabled older members.

Below are two examples of effective and ineffective confrontations:

Example 1

Ineffective Confrontation

"You are always complaining about your health. Can't you talk about anything else?"

Effective Confrontation

"I appreciate your telling me about how you are feeling when I visit. I really want to know how you are doing, but I also would like to spend our time together talking about other things as well. What do you think?"

Example 2

Ineffective Confrontation

"Who are you to tell me what to do? Do you have to butt into everything ?"

9. Caring Enough to Confront

Effective Confrontation

"I am irritated when you tell me how to spend my money. I appreciate your being concerned about me, but it is important to me that I manage it myself."

Caregivers can improve their confronting skills by thinking about their choice of wording **before** they confront. The exercise, "Confronting with Care" on page 78, will help caregivers practice making more effective confrontations.

Dealing with Impossible Situations

Sometimes life situations are almost unbearable. It is especially difficult communicating with a person in the later stages of Alzheimer's disease or other forms of dementia. Alzheimer patients often have extreme mood shifts, incoherent speech, and illogical behavior. Family caregivers of Alzheimer patients often suffer insomnia, irritability, and physical exhaustion. Effective communication is difficult in these situations.

Primary caregivers in these situations tend to become isolated from friends and neighbors. Financial strain and family tension leave the caregiver feeling trapped. The first step to coping in these cases is for caregivers to confront themselves: accept their limitations and seek regular assistance from other family members, friends, neighbors, and community resources. Professional counseling can offer valuable guidance in many cases.

10

FAMILY MEETINGS:
A COOPERATIVE EFFORT

Many families do not function as a cohesive unit even in times of crisis. One member--usually the primary caregiver--takes control, makes the decisions, and at some later date tells other family members what was done. Or the primary caregiver may talk with key family members individually before making decisions. Comments and suggestions are relayed to each person through the caregiver who acts as an information clearinghouse.

In the short run, these approaches may seem expedient, efficient, and effective. However, these kinds of decision-making processes can create problems later. The primary caregiver may be left in a difficult position relative to other family members.

First, the caregiver is in an uncomfortable position if the decisions made do not satisfy everyone. Other family members can criticize the decisions with the benefit of hindsight. Second, at some point the caregiver may need other family members to assist in the daily tasks of caregiving. Efficient actions from the primary caregiver may reinforce lack of involvement from other members. Soliciting help is easier when caregivers encourage family involvement from the beginning.

If at all possible, a face-to-face family conference should be held. Telephone conference calls can include relatives who live long distances from each other. Topics for family meetings include making appropriate living arrangements, making financial decisions, and allocating caregiving tasks.

Guidelines for Family Members

Collective family decisions are more successful if the following guidelines are followed:

1. **Always consider the needs and wishes of the older person.** In a crisis, family members may hastily search for solutions to problems without consulting the older person. The "efficient" way to resolve problems may not be the most appropriate or effective way. The decision may be a good one; however, if the dependent person does not play a central part in the decision-making process, he or she may put less effort into making it work.

> It was Dad's third stroke in the last year. That, plus arthritis, had left him an invalid with no hope for recovery. The doctor said he would require 24-hour nursing care. So while Dad was still in the hospital, my sister and I checked out all the nursing homes and found what we thought was the best place for him. It was between where we both lived and the staff seemed nice. We brought in some of his favorite things. We wanted to handle everything so he wouldn't have to worry about it.

> But when we told him everything was all set, he threw a fit. He said he wasn't "going to no nursing home!" Once he got there, he was awful to the staff and complained constantly about the other residents.

> We ended up telling him about two other nursing homes in the area which were possibilities. For some reason he decided he wanted to live in one on the other side of town. It didn't seem as nice to us, but at least it was his decision.

2. **Keep family members current regarding the level of care the older person requires.** Family members need time to understand the extent and nature of problems. Persons who are not told the potential severity of a situation do not respond well. Honest and open communication among family

members is important. While facing the truth can be painful, keeping secrets and hiding feelings can be more painful. Even young children need to be aware of the difficulties the family faces. People of all ages respond more positively to the known, rather than the hidden.

> I just wasn't prepared for it. I hadn't seen my grandmother for the entire semester. She was always heavyset. . . . She had a big lap to sit on as a child. . . . But now she's so small, so frail. I can't take it. I love her, she's my grandmother. But I can't stand to see her like that.

3. **Include all family members in the decision-making process.** The exclusion of individuals often leads to family war, mutiny or sabotage.

Family members are excluded for many reasons. Most often they live far away or have not been involved in previous decisions. Sometimes past rivalries stand in the way of open communication. In other cases, family members are "spared" having to be involved. These same persons may be the ones who later question the wisdom of decisions. Discontent surfaces and the primary caregiver suffers the added strain of family turmoil.

Family members generally appreciate an honest description of the situation and alternatives being considered. Seeking their opinions before a decision is made avoids later conflict. Past rivalries need to be set aside, at least temporarily. Relatives living far away can be contacted by telephone.

Some family members may not want to be involved in the care of an older person. Sometimes, these persons have unmet needs or past hurts which are not known or not understood by others in the family. Some members avoid caregiving responsibilities because they do not want to face the sad condition of a loved one becoming frail. Others may avoid caregiving because it reminds them of their own mortality. Most people will, however, help in caring for an older person if asked.

> My brother lives nearby but was frequently out of town on business. He visited two or three times a month, usually bringing a small gift to Mom. My older sister lives an hour away. She used to criticize me for leaving Mom alone sometimes during the day. My younger sister lived about twenty minutes away, but rarely visited. She said she couldn't stand to see Mom so frail.
>
> They were all surprised when I insisted on a family meeting. It was our first. The meeting was awkward and tense, especially in the beginning. After a lot of talking and some arguing, everyone agreed to help more.
>
> My brother agreed to schedule regular visits on weekends when I could visit friends or go shopping alone. He would even help Mom get ready for bed. My older sister accepted that Mom was capable of staying alone during the day for a few hours. She felt badly about not doing more and was taking out her frustration on me. She agreed that a weekly phone call to Mom would help her feel closer. During her vacation time, Mom could stay with her.
>
> My younger sister said she was intimidated by how I always handled everything. She was scared to be with Mom alone and felt she had little to offer Mom or me. We agreed to work out some times she could be with Mom when I was there.
>
> I think we all felt better after the meeting. I know I did.

4. **Set realistic goals.** In allocating caregiver tasks, allow persons time to consider what they are willing and able to do before they make definite commitments. With good intentions, family members volunteer to do anything to help an older person. Other family, work and community responsibilities limit what one can physically and emotionally manage. Difficult choices among commitments made to employers, children, spouses or parents usually produce guilt and ill-feelings. Primary caregivers who accept their own limitations can help others realize their limitations **before** they make promises.

5. **Be prepared to regroup and revise plans.** Life events such as births, deaths, illnesses, divorce and relocation affect the quantity and quality of family support available. As one solution is reached, life promises a change in circumstances--for better or for worse. The health status of older members can change radically within short periods of time. Problems may need to be redefined and additional alternatives explored. **Problem solving is not a single event, but a way of living.**

Professional groups are increasingly aware that they can best serve older adults by including their families. Medical and social services are more effectively administered when professionals and families work as partners in the overall care of a dependent older person. In some cases, professional persons may actually facilitate an initial family meeting. However, even under these situations of professional direction, the onus of responsibility lies with the individual family members working as a shared-functioning unit.

For some caregivers, the goal of a cooperative, mobilized family unit is a nice ideal, but is unrealistic for their circumstances. Mobilizing the family is more appropriate for some primary caregivers than for others. In many situations, deciding which family members should be included can be difficult. In situations of divorces and remarriages, family members may be uncertain where their loyalties and responsibilities are with regard to stepparents, stepbrothers, and stepsisters. In a few families, intense friction accumulated over many years may be more than the primary caregiver is emotionally or physically prepared to deal with. In these cases, the caregiver must decide the extent to which they will include other members, assessing both the advantages and disadvantages over the long run. It helps to face these issues before members are brought together in a crisis. Some caregivers may request the guidance of a professional family therapist to help the family deal with past issues as well as the present concerns of a frail or disabled member.

II. Understanding Relationships

For most, however, encouraging family involvement is an effective way to minimize the stress of the primary caregiver and to provide better care for the dependent older person. The "Family Caregiver Action Plan" on page 79 provides a structure for families to define problems, consider alternatives and make cooperative decisions.

ACTIVITIES

UNDERSTANDING RELATIONSHIPS

o Relationship Inventory

o Listening with Care

o Confronting with Care

o Family Caregiver Action Plan

RELATIONSHIP INVENTORY

How do you feel about . . .

	Uncomfortable			Comfortable	
	1	2	3	4	5
How you relate to your older relative?	1	2	3	4	5
How you relate to other people in your life?					
a. _____	1	2	3	4	5
b. _____	1	2	3	4	5
c. _____	1	2	3	4	5
d. _____	1	2	3	4	5
How you show love?	1	2	3	4	5
How you show anger?	1	2	3	4	5
How others "see" you?	1	2	3	4	5
How you take care of yourself?	1	2	3	4	5

What do you like most about your relationships?

_____

_____

What would you like to change in your relationships?

_____

_____

LISTENING WITH CARE

Set aside a special time with your older relative, free of distractions or interruptions. It can be for only a few minutes (5 to 20 minutes). Use effective nonverbal and verbal listening skills. Let the other person lead the conversation as much as possible.

After spending quality time with the person, consider the following questions:

1. How did your "special" conversation differ from "normal" conversations?

2. What did you learn from the conversation about the other person? About yourself?

3. How did you feel during the conversation? After the conversation?

4. When will you be able to set aside another "special" time?

5. Are there other family members or friends who could use your listening ear?

CONFRONTING WITH CARE

Confrontation invites change and growth in individuals and in relationships. Confrontation does not mean a person is selfish or is not accepting. It does mean a person is interested enough to look for improvements in situations. Effective confrontation comes from an empathetic attitude, simple speech and honest response.

1. Behavior: Describe in nonblameful terms a problem situation you have experienced recently or experience frequently.

2. Effect: Describe in specific, tangible terms how it affects you.

3. Feeling: How do you feel when the problem occurs? (If you feel anger, try to identify the feelings underlying the anger, such as frustration, embarrassment, or hurt.)

4. Now form a simple, honest confrontation statement including a nonblameful description of the behavior, how you feel, and how it affects you.

   Example: I am concerned (feeling) when you drive the car at night (behavior) and can't sleep until I know you have reached home safely (effect).

Note: When you confront a person, be ready to listen to their needs. The goal is to reach a mutually acceptable agreement.

FAMILY CAREGIVER ACTION PLAN:
DIRECTIONS

The Action Plan chart (pages 80 and 81) may be completed by an individual family member or by members in a family meeting.

Column 1: List the caregiving tasks and concerns of family members. You may wish to include caregiving needs which are currently being met but which need a "back-up" plan.

Column 2: List or describe ways in which the tasks/concerns are currently handled.

Column 3: List additional or alternative resources which might be useful for each task/concern. Resources would include people, information, agencies, and services.

Column 4: Identify advantages and disadvantages to alternative resources. Consider the difficulty or ease of accessing the resource.

Column 5: Write down your next step and who will be responsible for it. Next steps may involve physical activity, or they may be passive actions such as further discussion, additional thought, or prayerful meditation.

FAMILY ACTION PLAN

1	2	3
Tasks/Concerns	Current Situation	Alternatives

Activities for Part II

Date:

4	5	6
(Dis)Advantages	Next Step	Additional Notes

III

MAKING DECISIONS

Older persons and their families face major decisions involving health care, living arrangements, and financial and legal planning. This part gives an overview of the most common problems and possible alternatives. It suggests the needs for caregivers to explore further for answers relevant to their specific circumstances.

Chapter 11 looks at the role of the family in monitoring the health care of frail or ill members. Special emphasis is placed on the health of the primary caregiver. Chapter 12 gives the general types of housing alternatives for older adults. Chapter 13 suggests financial and legal considerations in planning for serious illness and death. In all cases, individuals are encouraged to seek professional medical, legal and financial assistance.

The last chapter, "Gaining Perspective," presents the author's personal thoughts on dealing with especially difficult situations. It is meant as encouragement, with the sincere hope that caregivers take care of their own physical, psychological, and spiritual well-being.

11

HEALTH CARE:
THE ROLE OF THE FAMILY

The family is the primary group in which preventive health behavior is encouraged or discouraged. Patterns of diet and exercise as well as underlying beliefs about oneself are developed in the family. Families promote good health care by encouraging regular physical examinations, immunization, balanced diets, exercise, and social activity.

Health Care for the Impaired Older Person

Health care providers assist in promoting quality care for older adults by giving their family caregivers accurate and adequate information. Family members need to understand the nature of and management of health problems. Trained health professionals who can serve as information sources for caregivers include nurses, physical therapists, nutritionists, and physicians.

Primary caregivers can assist older persons by assuring that accurate information is given to physicians. Individuals should keep a list of all prescriptions and over-the-counter medications taken, as well as any reactions or symptoms. Questions for physicians should be written down prior to appointments in order to avoid forgetting them later. The only "dumb" question is the one not asked.

Caregivers are better equipped to plan for and cope with physiological and mental changes in older persons if they understand the potential health problems and their warning signals. Family members should not hesitate to request specific information about the condition, symptoms, treatment alternatives, and side effects of treatments. The primary caregiver may need to be persistent in requesting frank and complete information on the health status of older family members. They can help the older person understand the condition and treatment. Frail or disabled persons often have difficulty taking prescribed medicines correctly. Sometimes childproof bottles are also elderproof. Adults of all ages do not always follow medication directions. The more medications taken, the greater chance for side effects and interference with one another. Caregivers can help monitor the prescribed and over-the-counter medicines taken. Physicians need to be aware of every kind of medicine the old person is currently taking.

The functional capacity and personal health of family members affect the demands on primary caregivers. Understanding the level of dependency of the older person is critical in determining the appropriate level of care and involvement from the caregiver. Not knowing the abilities and limitations of the older person could result in too little or too much assistance.

Old age is not a disease. Biological changes that occur in old age do, however, leave the body more vulnerable to disease. It is always important to look for the cause of any mental or physical change and, if possible, to treat it promptly. A decline in health should not be automatically dismissed as a normal part of aging.

Helen, who cared for her 82-year-old mother and 68-year-old husband, noticed a dramatic change in her own energy level. Her appetite dropped and she had lost considerable weight. She was sleeping more and at different times of the day. She frequently felt nauseous. Her doctor's initial response was that "these things happen when you get older" and "she should just take it easy."

Most people would probably have taken the doctor's advice and returned home sick. However, Helen, a nurse by training, knew that it was more than that. She insisted on a thorough examination. Results from tests revealed Helen had hepatitis, for which a medication was prescribed.

Many national health organizations such as the American Heart Association and the Arthritis Foundation have pamphlets on specific health problems. Some organizations offer educational programs and support groups for persons with health problems and their families.

Medical care for older adults is expensive. The means to pay for it are inadequate and the procedures for payment are complicated. Many adults believe Medicare pays for more than it actually does. Individuals need to understand the restrictions on Medicare payment. Many insurance companies offer "medi-gap"insurance, which is intended to pay for the difference between the medical costs and what Medicare pays. The coverage offered by medi-gap policies varies and needs to be carefully evaluated. Medicare, insurance, and hospital paperwork can be intimidating. Primary caregivers or other family members can assist older persons with confronting government agencies, insurance companies, and hospital procedures.

The Caregiver's Health

Medical problems of older adults are frequently multiple and chronic, posing greater physical, financial, and emotional burdens for their families. The most difficult part of taking care of a frail or disabled person is the emotional strain of learning to live with the physical and/or mental limitations. These hardships translate to enormous stress for the caregiver, who also becomes more vulnerable to disease and illness. Older spouse caregivers are most vulnerable to health problems. Many suffer from acute and prolonged illness, resulting in part from exhaustion.

Caregivers who face excessive demands are more likely to abuse or neglect their older relative. More than anything else, they need respite care--a chance to step away from the situation, to regain energy and perspective.

Caregivers serve their families better when they care for their own physical and psychological needs. They also encourage wellness in their families by modeling a healthy lifestyle in their own behavior. The "Healthy Lifestyle Checklist" on page 109 is appropriate for all family members.

In the concern for a frail or disabled older person, caregivers often overlook the need to prepare for their own possible illness or death. In the event of an emergency, arrangements need to be made for the care of the older person in the absence of the primary caregiver. This would include making available to a responsible person the information in "What Every Family Should Know" on page 111. Someone besides the caregiver needs to know practical information about the care of the older person.

Caregivers need to consider their own physical and psychological well-being. They cannot give what they do not have. The ability to care for another depends on one's own health. Family members can encourage the primary caregiver to live a healthy lifestyle by sharing in the caregiving tasks.

12

LIVING ARRANGEMENT ALTERNATIVES

One of the more difficult and disturbing decisions older adults face is choosing satisfactory living arrangements which are appropriate to their needs. Unfortunately, many older adults and their families do not begin to consider housing alternatives until the older person's ability to live independently is questioned.

Living arrangements which are the result of a conscious decision-making process will be more likely to be appropriate for the older person. Ultimately, satisfactory living arrangements reduce the stress for the primary caregiver and other family members, and add to the well-being of the older person.

The role of family members in deciding on living arrangements will vary depending on the abilities of the older adult. In some situations, particularly during an unexpected health crisis, the primary family caregiver may have to make independent decisions on behalf of the older person.

Older adults should be involved in all personal decisions to the fullest extent possible. Family caregivers should encourage older adults to make their own decisions when they are able. Relatives might assist in the decision-making process by gathering information and exploring alternatives with the older person, while at the same time being sensitive to the oider person's need to feel in control of the decision.

Moving wasn't easy for me. I lived alone and most of my close friends were dying. So I decided while I still had my health I should find a retirement apartment near my son and his family.

My daughter-in-law drove me to look at all the places, and my son checked out the room sizes and helped me decide what furniture would fit. But I made all the phone calls to the different apartments, compared services and rent, and made all the moving arrangements.

There were times I wanted my son and daughter-in-law to tell me what I should do. And I think I even got mad at them a couple of times because they wouldn't. I am so pleased, though. At least for now, I made the right decision.

My House or Yours?

Many families think their options are limited to "my house" or a nursing home. The reflexive response of caregivers to the housing needs of older family members is often an invitation to move in with them. Before the family has given it much thought, the words are out: "Why don't you come live with us?"

While sharing households with several generations can be mutually satisfying, it can also be mutually horrifying. Bringing an older person into the household usually changes family rountines and patterns. Family members may not feel the new arrangements are satisfactory.

The following are some questions which should be considered in deciding if an older family member should move in with the primary caregiver:

1. Do you get along with each other over long periods of time?

2. How do the other family members feel about the older person moving in? What would they each be expected to contribute to the care of the older member and support of the caregiver?

3. What practical adjustments would need to be made in terms of schedules, space, privacy, and financial costs?

4. Is this a long-term or short-term arrangement?

90

5. Can the planned living arrangements realistically meet the older person's physical and social needs?

6. What are other living arrangement alternatives?

Older men and women prefer to live independently in their own houses or apartments. This allows them more control over their lives. Simple decisions such as when to sleep and what to eat become very important when they are threatened by a change in living arrangements. A sense of independence and ownership is as important to older adults as it is for younger adults.

Housing Alternatives

The following is a brief description of living arrangements which address different dependency needs of older persons:

Family members can encourage older persons to live in their own homes by making simple home adjustments or seeking in-home community services for the older person. Simple **home modifications** can make living easier and safer for older persons. For example, family members can check for adequate lighting, secured rugs, stair rails, and smoke detectors. Emergency communication response systems are helpful for persons who live alone. In the event of an emergency, illness or accident, persons are able to contact help by pressing a single button.

The Arthritis Foundation and the American Heart Association are good sources of information about household gadgets available to increase the mobility and independence of disabled persons. These devices range from raised toilet seats, to velcro fasteners, to large-numbered clocks and telephones. They may help older adults to compensate for physical limitations and to continue living independent, satisfying lives in their own homes.

III. Making Decisions

Several **in-home services** are available which allow less-independent persons to remain in their homes. These programs include home-delivered meals, home health aids, friendly visitors, nutrition programs, and transportation. Family caregivers may want to investigate specific programs with the older person. Services provided by agencies do not replace family caregivers, but they do assist in overall care. Information about the availability and costs of these services in any community is possible through Area Agencies on Aging (AAA) or town social service departments. Completing the "Directory of Resources and Services" on page 110 will help older persons in their decisions.

Adult day care is a specialized program for people with physical and/or mental difficulties. It provides professional supervision in a social setting during the day for disabled or frail adults. Services typically include counseling, meals, health screening and socialization. Adult day care can provide older adults supervision when family caregivers are employed during the day.

Another option for older adults is **congregate housing**, which can provide support services for persons who can no longer live alone. Congregate housing facilities offer support services such as: (1) meals at a central location in the complex, (2) housekeeping assistance, and (3) personal assistance. Other services sometimes included are counseling, recreation, preventive health care, and transportation. Older persons living in these kinds of facilities are expected to be mobile and not require routine nursing care.

Continuing care facilities offer a range of living arrangements, from completely independent units to nursing homes. In many facilities, a substantial entrance fee and a monthly payment are required. Residents can move from one level of care to another within the complex if their needs change, depending on the availability of space.

12. Living Arrangement Alternatives

The need for **long-term care facilities** with full-time professional care of an older relative is sometimes necessary. Unfortunately, institutional care in hospitals and nursing homes is associated with failure of the family to "support its own." This generates feelings of abandonment for the older person and guilt for family members. For many caregivers the decision comes only after months of enormous physical and emotional strain.

After Dad died, Mother started having trouble remembering things. She would often forget where she was. The manager of the retirement building called me at work one day and told me Mother was picked up walking toward the expressway, and that she could not stay there any longer. I brought Mother home with me.

I fixed up a bedroom with all her favorite things--pictures, pillows, lamps. I would come home every day at noon to check on her. I made her special meals.

But no matter what, I couldn't please her. She would get angry because I had to go to work, and would say awful things to me. Sometimes sho would take too much of her medicine or leave the stove burners on. It got so bad, I just couldn't leave her alone. So I got my daughter to stay with her in the mornings, and my daughter-in-law to stay with her in the afternoon. But they couldn't keep doing that plus take care of their own families.

After two months of sleepless nights and exhausting days, I decided to check around for nursing homes, only to find out they all had long waiting lists. I thought I could take just about anything so Mother wouldn't have to go to a nursing home. Now I just have to take one day at a time . . . and do the best I can . . . and pray.

Less than 5% of persons over 65 are in nursing homes at any one time. Approximately 20% of people over 85 years old are in nursing homes, and about 30% of all people will spend some time in a nursing home. These figures suggest that nursing homes are the choice of last resort, but they are also an important alternative living arrangement. "Home" can be and is a nursing home for many older adults.

93

III. Making Decisions

The most difficult time for families is in actually making the decision and in admitting a relative into a nursing home. However, some families report renewed and strengthened closeness after a period of adjustment to the new setting.

Families do not give up their caregiving role once a member moves to a nursing home. Rather, they share in the caregiving with nursing home staff. Families continue to visit and contribute to the emotional and social needs of the older adult. Generally, the more involved the family is with the care facility in nontechnical aspects of caregiving, the more positive is the relationship between the older person and the family.

> I still visit Mother every day after work. We just sit together and maybe talk about the kids. I'll feed her some of her favorite Jello. My stomach turns inside out everytime she complains about wanting to go home. But it's still so much easier now, knowing I am not responsible for doing everything. It hurts seeing her so weak and helpless, but I know she is getting better care.

Once family members accept their limitations of dealing with the frail person's needs, feelings of guilt lessen and family relations among all members can improve. These are not easy decisions under any circumstance. The emotional level within the family can become so intense that decisions cannot be made objectively. Families are sometimes not able to assess the level of care needed. They may not know the alternatives available. It can help to consult an outside person, such as a social worker or a case manager, to assess the needs of the older person. This outside resource person may help in finding or determining the most viable living arrangements for the older adult. It also may help family relationships to have an outside person, an "expert," recommend a course of action.

The Reality of Long-Term Care Costs

The inability to pay for long-term care is one of the greatest hardships many older pesons and their families face.

94

12. Living Arrangement Alternatives

Government help through Medicaid pays for the very poor. The very wealthy can afford to buy good care. Unfortunately, for the vast majority of persons long-term care can deplete in a few months the modest savings accumulated over many years.

> After 45 years of hard work, scrimping, and saving, what do I have to show for it? Two years ago Lillian and I had our social security checks, a small pension, a house that was paid for, and $40,000 in savings. What more could anyone ask for? All our savings were used up in a little over a year to pay for the nursing home costs. Then I had to sell the house and move in with my daughter and her family. The money from the house will cover the nursing home costs for about 3 more years. Even if Lil got better, she couldn't come home. There's no place for her to stay.

The reimbursement procedures of Medicare and state and federal laws are complicated. Older adults and their families need to be aware of the correct regulations and the possible financial problems in order to plan in advance for long term care needs.

The problems of long-term care must be addressed on a national level. The responsibility lies with the middle generation to develop programs which will provide for the home care and long-term care needs of older persons.

13

LEGAL AND FINANCIAL
CONSIDERATIONS

Family members are often in the difficult situation of wanting to help an older person with legal and financial affairs but not wanting to interfere unnecessarily. Unfortunately, many caregivers face emergencies unprepared for serious illness or death. The information in this chapter is an overview of some of the issues family caregivers face in the event of incapacity or death of the older person.

Money: A Taboo Topic

Some individuals are more comfortable managing money than others. They are familiar with paying bills, applying for loans, preparing tax returns and dealing with government bureaucracies. Managing someone else's money is, however, very different from managing one's own. Older adults who have difficulty comprehending the effects of higher prices of goods and services sometimes complain about where the money is going. If an older adult, whose funds are being managed, has a lot of assets, the primary caregiver may sense more pressures of accountability from the older person or from other family members. If the older adult has limited assets, the demands on the primary caregiver's ability to stretch funds or to supplement funds with personal money are great.

Most families do not share specific information about their finances. Typically, men do not talk with women about money, and parents do not talk to children about this subject. Although women do most of the buying, they are often unaware of the family's overall financial picture. Wives who do not know the details of their personal financial affairs may have greater difficulty managing financing after the death of their husbands.

> You know, Anthony made all the decisions in our family. Every week he gave me money for groceries and odds and ends. I never paid any attention to the bills that came in. He took care of everything. I guess I thought when he died, I'd be able to find everything . . . or that things would sort of take care of themselves. It's actually embarrassing now, having to ask my son-in-law to explain things to me.

Talking about finances is less likely between parents and children than it is between spouses. Generational boundaries preclude either parents or adult children from discussing how much money they each have and how they are spending it. Both generations want to assure each other they are managing independently without the support or advice of the other. When financial assistance is extended, it is usually from the older to the younger generation. Reversing the giving, with the younger aiding the older, violates the parent's sense of what is appropriate. Sharing financial information is especially strained between an older father and his adult daughter. This violates both generational and gender boundaries.

Although talking about money can be stressful for family members, **not** talking about it can be more stressful. Caregivers need to assess their own family situations and determine how and to what extent they should be involved in financial matters of their older relatives. The extent of their involvement will vary according to the abilities of the older relative. Sometimes caregivers need to know certain financial information but do not want to intrude into the personal affairs of the older person. They respect the older person's autonomy over his financial affairs, but recognize signs of declining ability. The older person might overdraw the bank account, lose depositing checks, make unusual purchases, or forget to pay bills. If such occurrences are frequent, the caregiver may need to intervene.

It helps if the older person recognizes the need to share financial information, but this is not always the case. Caregivers need not feel guilty about bringing up the uncomfortable subject of money if they are motivated by a sincere desire to look after the welfare of the older person. Most family caregivers are not trying to "get the money" or "take control." Their intent is not to intrude, but rather to prepare for serious illness or death.

Preparing for Serious Illness

Caregivers are often unsure of when and how much assistance is needed. The decision to intervene in the financial affairs of an older person is based on the degree to which mental, physical, or emotional complications prevent the person from acting in his or her best interest. **The least restrictive or controlling action is the best.**

The following is a brief description of legal steps older adults and caregivers may take. They are listed in order of least restrictive to most restrictive. Since **laws and terminology** vary among states, **professional legal advice is essential.**

Older adults may have **joint bank accounts** with a family member. Joint accounts are arranged by signing a bank signatory card. This allows the caregiver to oversee the payment of bills and deposits. The most common problem with joint accounts with caregivers who are not spouses involves the trust of the caregiver. Other family members may question the use of funds and the "special" arrangement of the caregiver.

An adult of any age may use a **power of attorney** to grant a designated person the authority to make specific legal and/or financial decisions on his or her behalf. The general power of attorney may be revoked at any time by the grantor and become invalid if the grantor becomes incompetent. A **durable**

power of attorney remains in effect if the person later becomes incompetent.

An older adult may request **voluntary representation**, whereby the court appoints an individual to manage his or her affairs. Unlike the power of attorney, voluntary representatives are subject to the oversight of the court. Voluntary representatives are appointed without making a finding of incapacity of the older person.

There may be times when family members need to take control of the older person's financial and personal affairs. In these severe situations a **conservator** or **guardian** may be appointed by the probate courts. Family members are often appointed as conservator over an older person and/or his estate.

The legal procedures for a conservator require medical and/or psychiatric evidence of incapacity. Nontraditional lifestyles, personal neglect, or frivolous spending do **not** constitute incapacity if the person understands his actions and their consequences. Only when the adult does not understand his actions is he considered incapable. Actions which the family judges as foolish may be within the normal legal rights of the older person.

Anyone may file a petition of incapacity with the probate court. In some situations, such as with victims of Alzheimer's disease, families deny the severity of the condition and the need for legal action. Some families realize the severity but do not want to be the ones to bring an incompetency petition to the courts. Professionals such as doctors or social workers may file a petition with the probate court.

Under a conservatorship of persons, individuals lose all their rights to manage their affairs, including the right to vote, drive a car, or write a check. It is with good reason that families and courts use conservatorships cautiously.

13. Legal and Financial Considerations

Preparing for Death

Certain basic information is important to all primary caregivers in emergency situations. The stress surrounding a sudden illness or death of an older person is complicated by not being able to locate necessary information. The time to gather the information is **before** emergencies.

On page 111 is a list of "What Every Family Should Know." The information is important for all adult family members to share, not just older adults. Caregivers can complete the form for themselves and give it to their older relative. This may encourage a reciprocal exchange and keep the relationship more balanced. Sometimes an outside expert--a lawyer, a physician, or a book on the subject--may persuade an older person to prepare for serious illness or death.

Preparing for death includes letting family members know the extent of medical treatment desired in extreme circumstances. Most adults do not fear death as much as they fear dying. Life-sustaining measures such as respirators and intravenous feeding are frightening for those who would prefer to die without benefit of medical technology.

Family members are often asked to make the final decisions regarding medical treatment. The financial and emotional costs to families often increase during the last few months of an older person's life.

More people are signing **living wills**, which state a person's desire not to be given life-sustaining measures following serious illness if there is no reasonable expectation for a meaningful life. (A sample living will is on page 112.) However, living wills are not honored unless physicians, hospital policy, and family members agree. The instinct of family members and the training of medical professionals is to do whatever is possible to maintain life.

III. Making Decisions

In spite of legislation that strengthens the rights of dying persons, physicians and hospitals are pressured by liability suits and court decisions to maintain life at all costs. Family caregivers are often torn between wanting to end the suffering of an older person and not wanting the person to die. In these situations, living wills can make it easier for family members to decline final medical treatment.

Financial and legal questions are sensitive but critical topics to consider before a family crisis occurs. How older persons respond to discussion of money and property management varies. For some, the discussion may confront fears which no one wants to talk about. For others, the discussions are viewed as signs of the family's genuine interest and concern. Caregivers must be sensitive to the mental and physical condition of a frail or ill older person, as well as the symbolic meaning they may associate with giving up any personal control over money or property. Individual circumstances also require professional guidance from legal and financial specialists.

14

GAINING
PERSPECTIVE

[There is] a time to weep and a time to laugh. . . .
Ecclesiastes 3:4

Life is not always easy to understand. Sometimes events and problems are bigger than any one person. It may even seem that the only good alternative is to accept the losses and endure the pain.

Loss in life is inevitable and often increases in old age: the loss of physical stamina and good health; the loss of meaningful work; the loss of loved ones. Loss accompanies the demands of caregiving: the loss of time and energy; the loss of outside social contact; and sometimes the loss of hope.

When we feel the weight of the world, we can lighten our load by sharing the hardships and appreciating the joyous moments. This final chapter is intended to help family members gain perspective in times of loss by accepting the support from others, by taking advantage of the joys, and by relying on one's faith.

First, **allow others to show their love.** In times of loss, persons need to reach out for support. Strength comes from one's family, friends, and faith. Sometimes we don't receive the support needed because we are not receptive to it. By either asking or giving permission to others to share our pain, we may in turn be able to share their joys.

III. Making Decisions

My 76-year-old mother lives with and takes care of my 102-year-old grandmother. My role is really to support my mother, so I visit every weekend and try to help out. I would usually leave tense and depressed, emotionally and physically drained. I wanted to do more for both Mom and Grandmother but at the same time I dreaded every visit.

One day I asked my friend Kay to come with me. I hadn't wanted to bother her before. She's one of those people who are quick to listen and just as quick to laugh. By the end of our stay, a little bit of Kay rubbed off on all of us. She brought energy, love, and life to my mother and grandmother. I learned a lot that day. Mostly I learned none of us can do it on our own.

We can share our difficult moments with those who are outside the situation. Others may not bring solutions, but they can bring a fresh perspective and encouragement. The support of family and friends makes coping with caregiving problems less stressful. Caring for frail or disabled older persons can be a unifying experience, bringing people together in compassionate ways.

Second, **allow the joy in life to happen.** We gain pespective by building on our positive emotions--love, laughter, hope, faith, creativity and playfulness. These emotions prepare us to face the disappointments in life.

George Bernard Shaw wrote: "Life does not cease to be funny when people die any more than it ceases to be serious when people laugh." Even in times of mourning, fun and funny things happen. Just as we recognize and accept our grief, we can also accept those special joyous moments.

We were at home after the funeral service for Dad . . . you know, the time when you sit around feeling empty in spite of all the food people bring. Everyone was in the living room sharing their sympathies and offering support. I had followed Mom into the bedroom to look for something when I noticed the picture of Dad with his floppy hat standing next to a huge fake fish--Dad always was one for "fish" stories--all I said was "Remember that one?" Then

Mom and I started laughing. I had to close the door so the others wouldn't think we were disrespectful or insensitive.

We started exchanging other funny stories about Dad over the years, knowing we weren't "supposed" to be laughing. But for the moment it made his death--and his life--more meaningful and helped us gain perspective. I don't think I have ever felt closer to Mom. That very special moment set the tone for the years ahead when I would be looking after Mom.

Laughing should not be forced in serious or solemn moments. We need the courage to feel our loneliness, our fatigue, our depression. We need the courage to cry. However, we also need to appreciate the joy in life when it comes our way. Humor can emerge from stressful situations in many forms: a timely, funny comment; seeing the absurdity in impossible situations; and laughing at our mistakes. Golda Meir noted:

> I have always felt sorry for people afraid of feeling, of sentimentality; who are unable to weep with their whole heart. Because those who do not know how to weep do not know how to laugh either.

There are times things get so bad we "don't know whether to laugh or cry." Giving ourselves permission to laugh and cry keeps our outlook on life balanced and equips us to face ongoing challenges.

Finally, **persons with religious convictions can embrace their faith** during difficult times. Spiritual strength allows one to give and receive freely, to create and sustain caring relationships. Faith can bring peace of mind, which allows one to transcend the pain and sorrows in life.

> When Ed was diagnosed as having cancer in the gastro-intestines, I had no idea it would be so painful for him. There wasn't anything to do but make the most of each day and wait out some indefinite time. We had no idea how long we had before he would die. As I look back on it now, I know the only thing that kept us going was our faith in God to deliver us from the pain and suffering.

III. Making Decisions

> Often during the day I would sit by his bed . . . hold his hand . . . we would smile at each other . . . and then we would pray together. We gave thanks for the time we had together and prayed for the strength and understanding to endure the moment, knowing that the pain would eventually end.

Religious faith brings an affirmation of life that nourishes and celebrates relationships of selfless love. Often, it is in difficult times that we are most aware of those relationships.

Life is like a tapestry. Up close we can see only delicate and intricate threads, but at a distance it is a beautiful picture. A person caring for a frail or disabled older person may be among the delicate threads. With the help of love and laughter from family, friends, and other support people, one can gain strength and encouragement.

There are no easy solutions. However, with a fresh perspective may come the ability to see the larger picture.

ACTIVITIES

MAKING DECISIONS

o Problem Identification:
   Health, Housing, and Money

o Healthy Lifestyle Checklist
   for Caregivers

o Directory of Resources and
   Services

o What Every Family Should Know

o Living Will

PROBLEM IDENTIFICATION: HEALTH, HOUSING, AND MONEY

1 a. To what extent is the health condition of your older relative a problem for you?

    Some ___ Considerable ___ Great ___

  b. Please describe the problem:

  c. What assistance or information do you need from others?

2 a. To what extent are living arrangements for your older relatives a problem for you?

    Some ___ Considerable ___ Great ___

  b. Please describe the problem:

  c. What assistance or information do you need from others?

3 a. To what extent are financial concerns of your older relative a problem for you?

    Some ___ Considerable ___ Great ___

  b. Please describe the problem:

  c. What assistance or information do you need from others?

HEALTHY LIFESTYLE CHECKLIST
FOR CAREGIVERS

Physical Wellness

___ 1. Do you exercise every day within your physical limitations?
___ 2. Do you allow time every day for relaxation?
___ 3. Do you smoke?
___ 4. Are you 10 pounds overweight? underweight?
___ 5. Do you eat a balanced diet?
___ 6. Do you watch your intake of caffeine, sugar, salt, and fats?
___ 7. Do you have regular physical exams, including dental care, breast exams, pap smears, and eye examinations?
___ 8. Do you fasten your seat belt when you drive?

Psychological Wellness

___ 1. Do you feel guilty when you say no?
___ 2. Do you have a friend you can confide in?
___ 3. Do you rely on pills or alcohol for depression or anxiety?
___ 4. Are you presently worried about something in the future?
___ 5. Are you presently feeling guilty about something in the past?
___ 6. Do you constantly seek the approval of others?
___ 7. Do you have an activity each day that has meaning for you?
___ 8. Can you laugh at your mistakes?

Resolution:

For a healthier life, I will _____

_____

_____

DIRECTORY OF
RESOURCES AND SERVICES

Services and resources vary among communities. Since access to services is not centrally coordinated it is sometimes difficult to identify what is available. Information sources include town social service departments, senior centers, area agencies on aging, visiting nurses associations, churches/synagogues, and telephone directories. Find out the services in your community. Include eligibility requirements and costs.

Available Services /   Contact Person/Phone #

1. Meal services (i.e., Meals on Wheels, nutrition sites)

2. Homemaker and house-keeping services

3. Personal and nursing care (i.e. visiting nurses, private nursing services)

4. Day care, senior centers

5. Companionship, friendly visitors, telephone reassurance

6. Transportation

7. Information and referral services

8. Family support: respite care, legal assistance, hospice, support groups

9. Other:

WHAT EVERY FAMILY SHOULD KNOW

Names and Phone Numbers of:
    Clergy: _____
    Doctor: _____
    Lawyer: _____
    Accountant: _____
    Insurance agent: _____
    Executor of your estate: _____

Location of:
    Will: _____
    Insurance policy: _____
    Bank books: _____
    Stock/mutual funds/investments: _____
    Checking and savings accounts: _____
    Safety deposit box: _____
    Mortgages/deeds: _____
    Birth certificate/marriage certificate: _____

Social security number: _____
Armed services serial number: _____
Insurance policy numbers: _____

Funeral and burial requests: _____
_____
_____
_____
_____
_____
_____
_____
_____
_____

III. Making Decisions

SAMPLE LIVING WILL

To My Family, Physician, Lawyer

Death is as much a reality as birth, growth, maturity and old age--it is the one certainty of life. If the time comes when I can no longer take part in decisions for my own future, let this statement stand as an expression of my wishes and directions, while I am still of sound mind.

If at such a time the situation should arise in which there is no reasonable expectation of my recovery from extreme physical or mental disability, I direct that I be allowed to die and not be kept alive by medications, artificial means or "heroic measures." I do, however, ask that medication be mercifully administered to me to alleviate suffering even though this may shorten my remaining life.

This statement is made after careful consideration and is in accordance with my strong convictions and beliefs. I want the wishes and directions here expressed carried out to the extent permitted by law. Insofar as they are not legally enforceable, I hope that those to whom this Will is addressed will regard themselves as morally bound by these provisions.

DURABLE POWER OF ATTORNEY (optional)

I hereby designate_____ to serve as my attorney-in-fact for the prupose of making medical treatment decisions. This power of attorney shall remain effective in the event that I become incompetent or otherwise unable to make such decisions for myself.

Optional Notarization:	Signed_____
"Sworn and subscribed to	Date_____
before me this____day	
of_____, 19_____."	Witness_____
_____	Witness_____
Notary Public	

For additional information about your state's laws regarding living wills, contact: Concern for Dying, 250 West 57th Street, New York, NY 10107.

SUGGESTED READING

Cohen, D., & Eisdorfer, C. The Loss of Self: A Family Resource for the Care of Alzheimer's Disease and Related Disorders. New York: W. W. Norton, 1986.

Deedy, J. Your Aging Parents. Chicago: Thomas More Press, 1984.

Edinberg, M. A. Talking with Your Aging Parents. Boston: Shambhala, 1987.

Hooyman, N. R. Taking Care: Supporting Older People and Their Families. New York: Free Press, 1986.

Horne, J. Caregiving: Helping an Aged Loved One. Glenview, IL: Scott, Foresman, 1985.

Mace, N. L., & Rabins, P. V. The 36-Hour Day: A Family Guide to Caring for Persons with Alzheimer's Disease, Related Dementing Illnesses and Memory Loss in Later Life. New York: Warner Books, 1981.

Porcino, J. Growing Older, Getting Better: A Handbook for Women in the Second Half of Life. Reading, MA: Addison-Wesley, 1983.

Shelley, F. When Parents Grow Old. New York: Harper & Row, 1988.

Silverstone, B., & Hyman, H. K. You and Your Aging Parents:The Modern Family's Guide to Emotional, Physical, and Financial Problems. New York: Pantheon Books, 1982.

INDEX

Index